ZELDA

*"In dedication to Malcolm Nightfire Treadwell and everyone else on their
lifelong quest. May your hearts remain full, your aim remain true and may
you never give up. We all have our links to the past."*
Sterling Treadwell

*Zelda. The History of a Legendary Saga. Volume 2:
Breath of the Wild*
by Valérie Précigout
Published by Third Éditions
32 rue d'Alsace-Lorraine, 31000 Toulouse
contact@thirdeditions.com
www.thirdeditions.com

Follow us:
🐦 : @Third_Editions
📘 : Facebook.com/ThirdEditions
💬 : Third Éditions
📷 : Third Éditions

Edited by: Nicolas Courcier and Mehdi El Kanafi
Editorial assistants: Damien Mecheri and Clovis Salvat
Texts by: Valérie Précigout
Proofreading: Christophe Delpierre and Zoé Sofer
Layout: Delphine Ribeyre
Covers: Frédéric Tomé
Translated from French by: Keith Sanders (ITC Traductions)

This educational work is Third Éditions' tribute
to the game *The Legend of Zelda: Breath of the Wild.*

The author presents an overview of the history
of *The Legend of Zelda: Breath of the Wild* game in this one-of-a-kind volume that lays out
the inspirations, the context and the content of this title titles through original analysis and discussion.

English edition, copyright 2018, Third Éditions.
All rights reserved.
ISBN 978-2-37784-040-3

Valérie Précigout

ZELDA

THE HISTORY OF A LEGENDARY SAGA
VOLUME 2: BREATH OF THE WILD

03.rd

THIRD
éditions

ZELDA

THE HISTORY OF A LEGENDARY SAGA
VOLUME 2: BREATH OF THE WILD

PREFACE

HOUGH video games are widely perceived, even today, as a relatively new form of entertainment, the medium already boasts a number of series that have existed for thirty years and influenced entire generations of players. Among these long-standing franchises, *The Legend of Zelda* is remarkable in that it has managed to maintain its initial freshness throughout its long history, without ever forgetting the importance of welcoming new players to the series. Its reputation has continued to grow with each passing year, so that today, it is universally recognized as one of the most sacred symbols in video gaming. While the first name we associate with Nintendo may be *Mario*, the company's image has been shaped just as much by the many contributions that the *Zelda* franchise has made to a medium that had never seen anything like its unique blend of action, adventure and RPG gameplay when it appeared on the scene in 1986.

Offering players an astounding degree of freedom at a time when "open world" games had not yet been invented, *The Legend of Zelda* for the FDS (Famicom Disk System) and NES (Nintendo Entertainment System) laid the groundwork for a saga that was logically oriented toward exploration, placing an equal emphasis on thrilling outdoor exploration and claustrophobic dungeon raids. But in hindsight, we can see that the concept proposed in the first *Zelda* game gradually became more restricted as the series went on, following a general tendency to sacrifice freedom of exploration for a more richly structured narrative.

Thirty years later, however, the situation has changed. Game developers now seek a return to the industry's roots, guided by a touch of nostalgia for the old ways—a change in perspective that has affected a number of different franchises.

With *The Legend of Zelda: Breath of the Wild*, Nintendo seeks to break free of the various limits that the series has imposed on itself over the years and attempts to fully realize the saga's original vision with help from the latest in video game technology. These ambitions go far beyond all the smaller step-by-step innovations offered in earlier episodes, which seemed to have lost sight of the 1986 game's original intentions in terms of pure freedom.

On March 3, 2017, the *Zelda* saga reached a symbolic turning point with the release of this new episode for Wii U and Nintendo Switch, kindling equal parts fascinated interest and apprehension in the hearts of all those who had followed, supported, and sometimes grown frustrated with the series over its thirty years of existence.

Valérie Précigout

Better known by her pseudonym Romendil, Valérie spent 15 years as a journalist for *Jeuxvideo.com*, Europe's largest video game website. A fan of Japanese RPGs, she managed to establish herself as an online critic when the Internet was still struggling to keep up with print media. She loves manga culture and Japanese leisure activities and shares her impressions about video-gaming news at *Extralife.fr*. She is also the author of *Dragon Ball: The Tribute*, from the Force label at Third Éditions, and contributes articles to the *Level Up* book series from the same publisher.

ZELDA

THE HISTORY OF A LEGENDARY SAGA

VOLUME 2: BREATH OF THE WILD

CHAPTER ONE

CREATION

TARTING production on a title that sought to radically redefine the core elements of a franchise as iconic as *The Legend of Zelda* involved a certain amount of risk for Nintendo. To fully understand the situation, we feel it is essential to start by determining what was really at stake in this challenging effort by looking at the many promises that *The Legend of Zelda: Breath of the Wild* carried with it from the earliest announcement of its development until the moment it was released. With this perspective in mind, we will first step back in time to examine any clues potentially found in other recent installments of the franchise as to the creators' desire to rethink the game's most basic conventions. We will then consider what fans were expecting from this attempt to go back to basics and revive the ambitions of the original *Legend of Zelda*. We will also look at Nintendo's communications strategy by way of the trailers and other official presentations that were used to introduce the game, and consider the credibility of *Breath of the Wild*'s claim to innovation in its approach to the open world genre. Of course, we will also focus considerable attention on director Hidemaro Fujibayashi's history with the series, and listen to the development team's thoughts as we attempt to better understand the origins of this latest *Zelda* game. We then close the chapter with a look at initial reactions from fans and video game journalists when the game was first released on March 3, 2017.

QUESTIONING OLD HABITS

A DESIRE FOR CHANGE

Well before the first hints trickled out about the production of *The Legend of Zelda: Breath of the Wild*, an episode that would attempt to redefine the saga's most basic conventions, certain early signs of this desire to break free from past routines had already begun to appear in recent iterations of the franchise. After the release of *The Legend of Zelda: Twilight Princess*, producer Eiji Aonuma continued his tireless search for ideas on how to liberate the series from a linear structure that had become increasingly restrictive. After all, there's no denying that, even in the eyes of its most zealous defenders, the rigid formula applied to each episode meant that each new installment held fewer surprises than the one before. If we started from the first game and drew a diagram of how Link's adventures have been organized over the years, we would see that the alternation of overworld exploration and dungeon sections has solidified into an unchanging and all-too-repetitive framework. In particular, while the need to find the hidden treasure in each temple to get hold of the key to the boss's lair is certainly one of the most distinctive and essential elements of the *Legend of Zelda*, it's no longer enough to satisfy players who have been doing it for years. Similarly, the standard cycle of moving the plot forward in the villages before heading forth into a new hostile region of the game and taking down its ruler feels a bit too much like what you'd find in any old JRPG. And finally, the constant recurrence of certain key symbols seems to underline this reluctance to consider even the slightest change—as reflected in the unchanging image of our hero, instantly recognizable by his green tunic and his legendary silence. As a result, what once defined the essence of a *Zelda* now seems less and less unique, and the regular addition of new gameplay elements is no longer enough to refresh a formula that seems in urgent need of a modern update. Even so, the teams at Nintendo didn't seem quite ready to abandon such a well-established approach and start over from scratch, which is why the evolution that we had seen since the release of *Twilight Princess* had been slow and progressive.

While the arrival of two consecutive episodes for the Nintendo DS, *Phantom Hourglass* (2007) and *Spirit Tracks* (2009), seemed to reflect a desire to explore new gameplay routines more than an attempt to restore the lost sense of freedom and exploration that had defined the first *Zelda*, the following episodes chose the opposite approach. In *The Legend of Zelda: Skyward Sword*, which came out on the Wii in 2011, the action takes place in a wide-open sky world designed to give players a truly exhilarating sense of freedom... at least in theory. In fact, though, players soon realized that this freedom of movement is only an illusion, and that the progression scheme is designed to guide them along a linear path from one floating island to the next, with no real ability to explore wherever they like. Nor does anything truly unexpected usually happen during Link's airborne travels, which amount to little more than quick rides on a Loftwing, the species of flying steeds that appear in the game. In this sense, exploring the sky in *Skyward Sword* is quite similar to exploring the ocean world of *The Wind Waker*: while players certainly had the option in that game to sail the seas as they pleased, the ocean's main role was simply to connect the islands to one another, but with no real sense of a unified world. To be sure, this bold feature did succeed in blurring the line between indoor and outdoor environments to create a more effective illusion of exploring a world with few fixed boundaries. But for Eiji Aonuma, it wasn't nearly enough. The producer himself spoke of his inability to establish a real connection between the floating islands in *Skyward Sword*, and of his sense that rather than bringing coherence to the world of the game, the islands made it feel more fragmented than ever. This was a key turning point in Aonuma's thought process, as he came to clearly reject the idea of building another game around design principles that were the opposite of an open world.

Another notable attempt to establish new modes of progression in a *Zelda* game can be seen in *A Link Between Worlds*. This reimagining of the episode from the SNES era, released for the 3DS in 2013, introduces a radical change in the way players can approach the adventure. Thanks to a rabbit-eared traveling merchant named Ravio, Link can simply rent virtually any of the key items he needs throughout his quest. This includes all of the series' best-known secondary weapons, including the Bow, the Hookshot, and the all-important Bomb Bag, which are usually essential for completing the dungeon trials, and which were previously found only in carefully guarded chests. Allowing players to get their hands on whatever items they find most useful for their quest, starting from a very early point in the game, is a clear sign of the producer's desire to break free of the classic linear structure and start moving toward more freedom of exploration. In *A Link Between Worlds*, players have more independence, and are no longer required to go through the dungeons in a specific and predefined order to get their hands on the one artifact that will open up further progression. Although this episode does include a certain number of restrictions intended to prevent players from completely sabotaging the challenge of the game—such as the requirement to buy items again if Link is killed, and to avoid emptying the endurance meter each time he uses one of these items—this new feature seems to be highly effective in changing the overall dynamic of the game. The ability to rent any item gives players a strong incentive to explore all the secrets hidden around the edges of the main adventure and outside of the dungeons— much like the first *Zelda* game, in which (to take one example) players could buy a candle from a merchant hidden in a cave and start burning down trees right from the beginning of the game!

Given all this, it's hard to argue that Nintendo never looked for ways to change the series' longstanding routines, even if these early attempts were also met with criticism from players who saw them as mere inconveniences. In the case of *Skyward Sword*, for example, the originality of a world built among the clouds often takes a back seat to the difficulties of controlling the sword with the Wii Motion Plus (an accessory that reproduces the movements of the Wiimote more quickly and precisely)—when it's not the game's infamously sluggish start that stands out most vividly in players' minds. Similarly, a fan of the 3DS episode *A Link Between Worlds* is unlikely to mention how renting items leads to greater freedom of exploration without first highlighting the game's other most unique feature: Link's ability to merge into wall paintings in environments, making skillful use of the 3D environments which were possible with the console. Although it is surely one of the game's best features, fans' lack of appreciation for this handheld episode clearly reflects their desire to see the franchise explore more ambitious possibilities. Often shunned for its low level of difficulty and short play time, this reinterpretation of the unforgettable *A Link to the Past*, timed to celebrate the twentieth anniversary of that game's release on the SNES, ultimately failed to excite the gaming public. It would apparently take more than a colorful homage to one of the most popular chapters in the series to rekindle the flame in the hearts of true *Zelda* fans, who were hoping to relive the excitement of a major event like the release of *Ocarina of Time*. And as the controversy over the cartoon-like design of *The Wind Waker* had shown a few years earlier, players also wanted to experience a more mature *Zelda* game, intended for a generation of grown-up gamers who had already had plenty of time to explore other, less time-worn approaches to game design—including open world games. In other words, if the *Zelda* series was going to make a change, it should be major and uncompromising—no more half-measures like the ones Nintendo had been offering up for thirty years.

THE DANGERS OF OVEREXPLOITING THE FRANCHISE

In hindsight, we can see that despite the risks that they represented for Nintendo at the time, these bold attempts to take the series out of its comfort zone by breaking with its well-worn routines and classic structure did not make much of an impression on players. One reason is that, beyond these considerations, fans have been especially concerned with the publisher's tendency to overexploit the franchise over the past fifteen years. Players had learned to await the arrival of each new *Zelda* game like the coming of the Messiah—but starting in the 2000s, the release schedule started to accelerate, and began to include second-tier installments like *Four Swords Adventures* and various spin-offs that were not always appreciated by *Zelda* purists. How many people still remember *Freshly-Picked Tingle's Rosy Rupeeland*, released on the DS in 2007—or its sequel, which was never distributed outside of Japan? It's not that these games were necessarily bad, but choosing the most off-kilter character in the franchise to star in the first real spin-offs from the *Zelda* saga didn't do much to impress players who were looking for serious adventure.

It's not surprising, then, that the appearance of *Link's Crossbow Training* for the Wii, a simple collection of challenges that let players use their Wiimote as a crossbow, also failed to arouse much enthusiasm in 2007. All the more so since seeing the saga's main hero appear in such a small-scale production—the primary purpose of which was to promote a new accessory for the Wiimote—was beginning to seriously taint the *Zelda* brand, and to undermine the credibility of these outings on the sidelines of the main saga.

So when Nintendo announced that Omega Force, a studio specializing in mass beat 'emups like the *Dynasty Warriors* series (published by Koei Tecmo), would be developing a fighting game featuring iconic characters from the *Zelda* saga for release on the Wii U in 2014, few believed that the project would be a success. Entitled *Hyrule Warriors*, the new game risked puncturing the sacred aura of a wildly popular series that had managed to maintain a virtually spotless reputation up to that point. Whether or not you like the concept behind the game—which is admittedly filled with good ideas, but confined to the usual limits of an Omega Force production—an important line had clearly been crossed. From that point on, players knew that the *Zelda* name could also be associated with second-tier productions that turned out to be highly opportunistic in some cases, and that Nintendo condoned such uses of the license, as abusive as they sometimes seemed to be. The 2016 release of *Hyrule Warriors Legends* on 3DS, an altogether respectable handheld version of the Wii U title which put all of its genuinely new content into paid DLC, tends to confirm this impression even more strongly.

In almost no time, the *Zelda* series had been shamelessly subjected to a dangerous level of overexploitation—not unlike the excesses of certain other major Nintendo licenses, with *Mario* chief among them. The number of titles in every possible genre featuring the company's biggest star in sports competitions or party games has increased so much in recent years that you'd be forgiven for forgetting that *Super Mario* was originally a series of platformers! The emphasis in the *Mario* series has changed so completely that canonical installments (like *Super Mario Odyssey* on the Nintendo Switch) are now considered a rare treat within their own family of games. Between the release of *Odyssey* and the last "real" *Mario* game before it, namely *Super Mario 3D World* in 2013, the mustachioed plumber had time to take a spin in a go-kart (*Mario Kart 8*), battle with friends (*Super Smash Bros. for Wii U*), play tennis (*Mario Tennis Ultra Smash*), party games (*Mario Party 10*), puzzle games (*Mario vs. Donkey Kong: Tipping Stars*) and RPGs (*Paper Mario: Color Splash*), and even put out his own level editor (*Super Mario Maker*) and participate in the Olympics twice with *Mario & Sonic at the Sochi Winter Olympics* in 2014, and a *Rio* version in 2016!

In that same year, he also appeared on smartphones for the first time in *Super Mario Run*, between two quick appearances on the 3DS (*Mario Party: Star Rush* and *Mario Sports Superstars*). As long as the game-buying public stays interested, Nintendo is happy to keep going back to the well again and again—

and never mind the critics who worry that new generations of players will buy the new spin-off titles without ever checking out the leading titles in the series.

Once considered to be the gold standard for all platforming games, *Mario* is now primarily an ultra-versatile pop culture character who no longer insists on perfection in every outing. The era when fans looked forward to each new game in the series as a historic event (*Super Mario World, Super Mario 64*) seems to have passed. With such a mind-boggling number of spin-offs of all kinds, it's no longer surprising to see the average review scores for *Mario* games appearing in the "good" range more often than receiving the excellent scores from younger years when the high-jumping plumber didn't spread himself quite so thin. Even the sports-based spin-offs that do get good reviews (like *Mario Kart, Mario Golf* and *Mario Tennis*) have gradually lost some of their luster, to the detriment of the original series' reputation. Given this history, it's not unreasonable to worry about the same type of scenario arising with the *Zelda* franchise. Of course, there have only been a few spin-off episodes so far, but the current trend suggests there are likely to be more—especially since Nintendo has opened another Pandora's box by offering DLC for a title like *Hyrule Warriors*, raising the specter of future *Zelda* games fragmented into small pieces of paid content. This development also affects *Breath of the Wild*, as we will see a bit later.

RETHINKING CONVENTIONS

EIJI AONUMA'S MESSAGE

Eiji Aonuma revealed that the desire to break out of the usual progression patterns associated with the various games in the series went all the way back to *The Legend of Zelda: Skyward Sword*. The fact that exploring the world in this episode involved traveling through the sky had the unfortunate side effect of making the world feel fragmented and incoherent. The producer felt that preventing players from roaming freely on foot over the paths connecting the different regions of the game would be a legitimate source of frustration, and many people's reactions to the game seemed to prove him right. Critics of this design wanted to know what lay behind this lack of unity in the world. Shouldn't there be something to explore even between the zones actually presented in the game? It was time to take a decisive step: the *Zelda* saga would have to have its own open world. Of course, Nintendo would first have to be sure that the Wii U was up to the task of reproducing a viable open world that would bring back nostalgic memories of exploring the first *Zelda* game without making players wait for loading screens. After careful study, it seemed that an open world with a fluid gameplay experience was indeed a real possibility—an idea that Aonuma had been playing with since the days of *The Wind Waker*.

It had become urgent for Nintendo to prove to its fans that, even after thirty years, the franchise still had ambitions that were worthy of its lofty reputation. Ultimately, Eiji Aonuma chose a video message on the Nintendo Direct online broadcast of January 23, 2013, to let the world know that the next *Zelda* game for the Wii U would focus on totally rethinking the core conventions of the series. The brevity of the message confirmed—for anyone who didn't already suspect it—that the original creators of the series, including Shigeru Miyamoto, were also struggling with a troublesome sense of fatigue toward a formula that had been set in stone for far too long. These concerns, which had previously seemed confined to the grumbling of worried fans, now felt almost like an admission of failure on Nintendo's part. *Zelda* was getting older, and it was time to guide the series in a new direction, even if it meant pushing it out of its comfort zone—no matter what the traditionalists might say.

In concrete terms, Aonuma promised an episode that would surprise players by breaking free of the codes that had governed virtually every game in the series since the very beginning. For example, players would no longer be required to explore dungeons in a predefined order—and they wouldn't necessarily have to play the game alone, either. According to Aonuma, there was no reason for these elements to be set in stone if it meant preventing the series from evolving in new and exciting directions. *The Legend of Zelda* would have to adapt to today's players, whose interests clearly differ at times from those of the past. Aonuma added that his teams had already tried to work on these types of challenges during the development of *Skyward Sword*, but without managing to break out of the linear structure of the game. However, he argued that the next *Zelda* game, the full name of which was still unknown at the time, would be able to achieve that goal and go back to basics with a return to the ideals of the first installment in the series.

These enigmatic statements hinted at a renewal that had been a long time coming for this franchise, which now finally seemed ready to take any risk necessary to rebuild its reputation by shaking up its established codes. While those codes had served as the basic recipe for the series throughout its history, they sorely needed to be dusted off and updated—without losing sight of what defined the soul of the *Zelda* saga. Of course, the results of this effort remained to be seen, but the producer's message was a call to arms that reflected a commendable desire to move forward.

A RETURN TO FREEDOM

This message gave new insight into why Eiji Aonuma, as the heir to the *Zelda* saga, considered it so important to restore the spirit of freedom that had gradually been lost in recent episodes, replaced by an increasingly rigid and linear structure. Of course, this renewed focus on freedom was clearly also driven by the growing worldwide popularity of open world games, by then the most popular genre on PS3, Xbox 360, PS4, and Xbox One consoles and on PC, in which the main story almost takes a back seat to the wide variety of side quests and other activities available to explore. As long as the overall world of a game feels like more than just pretty scenery, any player who's even the slightest bit receptive to its basic design will find it difficult to resist the call of exploration in a seemingly unlimited world.

By definition, an open world game is distinguished by a completely open-ended approach to level design. In other words, it is designed to let players run free in a world unconstrained by invisible or artificial boundaries, in which they can move from one zone to another with no immersion-breaking loading screens. The transitions between different areas of the game are carefully concealed, to the point of disappearing completely—as opposed to most other games, which are based on a linear level design and a more fragmented world structure. It took a few major technological advances in recent years to bring us open world games truly worthy of the name (*The Elder Scrolls: Skyrim*, *Grand Theft Auto IV* and *V*, *Red Dead Redemption*, *Just Cause 3*, *The Witcher 3*, etc.), but the first open worlds date back to the 1980s, with pioneering games like *Elite* and *Ultima* on early microcomputers. The *Zelda* series, on the other hand—except for the first episode, which did capture this sense of free exploration—was quite clearly aligned with the category of games based on a linear approach to level design, in which players have to follow a more or less rigidly predefined path to reach the end of the adventure. They are not free to explore wherever they like at any point in the game and have to wait to acquire certain specific items to gain access to new areas. Their progression is subject to strict constraints of the type we find in the vast majority of recent action/adventure games. For a long time, this approach was considered the norm. But with the advent of open world games and players' instant infatuation with this new genre, it seemed inevitable that older approaches to level design would be called into question.

THE MAN AT THE CONTROLS

Now all that remained was to find someone who could take on the immense challenge of giving *Zelda* a new look. Producer Eiji Aonuma chose a man by the name of Hidemaro Fujibayashi as the director of *Breath of the Wild*. While the general gaming public knew little of this man in the shadows, whose name is generally eclipsed by those of bigger media personalities like Miyamoto and Aonuma, connoisseurs of the series knew that Fujibayashi had been working on *Zelda* games for a long time. His first contributions to the world of video games date back to 1995, when he was hired by Capcom as a planner for an interactive film and a mahjong game for 32-bit consoles (PlayStation, Saturn, and even the 3DO for the mahjong game). He later worked as the director for *Magical Tetris Challenge*, a puzzle game featuring Disney characters released on the Nintendo 64 and Game Boy Color in 1998.

In 2001, Capcom's history became intertwined with Nintendo's when the companies joined forces for an ambitious project to develop a series of six *Zelda* games for the Game Boy Color (see *Zelda. The History of a Legendary Saga. Volume 1*). More precisely, it was the independent company known as Flagship, founded by Capcom, Nintendo, and SEGA in 1997, that was in charge of the project. The original idea was to develop a remake of the first *Zelda* game for the GBC, along with several original titles. But as the project expanded uncontrollably in the face of tight deadlines, the development team decided to limit itself to just three games that would work together as a "Triforce Trilogy". The most unique feature of these games would be their interactions with each other, with actions taken in any one of the three games having an effect on the two others. Ultimately, the planned trilogy was reduced to just two titles, but the idea of interactions among games was preserved in the form of a password that could be used to connect the two adventures, leading to an ultimate confrontation with Ganon.

The two games were released simultaneously on Game Boy Color in 2001 under the titles *The Legend of Zelda: Oracle of Seasons* and *Oracle of Ages*. It was the first time in the history of the franchise that Nintendo had delegated the development of a *Zelda* game to another company—and it also gave Hidemaro Fujibayashi the chance to take his first steps as a director on the series. His role on these two games was initially to gather the ideas suggested by the development team and present them to producer Shigeru Miyamoto for approval. He was then named director and co-writer as he worked closely with the rest of the team on developing the story. The password system that tied the conclusions of the two games together was also his idea.

From 2001 to 2017, Fujibayashi continued to work on the *Zelda* franchise as a director for most of the episodes developed for handheld consoles: *Four Swords* (in 2002) and *The Minish Cap* (in 2004) for the Game Boy Advance, then *Phantom Hourglass* for the DS in 2007. With the latter title, Fujibayashi finally joined Nintendo's ranks, as Capcom had just shut down the Flagship studio for good. He was rewarded for his work in 2011 with the release of *Skyward Sword*, his first *Zelda* project for a home console, after five years of development. The next project that Eiji Aonuma would entrust to him would eventually be known as *Breath of the Wild.*

In a long interview with the British magazine *EDGE*, which devoted a full ten pages to the release of *The Legend of Zelda: Breath of the Wild* in its April 2017 issue, Hidemaro Fujibayashi shared a number of behind-the-scenes details about the game's design process. As a big fan of the first game in the series, the director explained that the roots of the new *Zelda* game were based in the idea of surviving in an environment with no limits. Exploration in *Breath of the Wild* would include the ability to reach any point in the world by climbing the mountains and gliding freely from one region to another. Another equally fundamental point was the need to make use of the resources provided by a unified and coherent environment, right down to details like using twigs as kindling to make a campfire—a perfect example of the type of gameplay the director wanted to include. From Fujibayashi's point of view, the best part of the *Zelda* saga was its puzzle game aspect. So he felt it was essential that his game provide fertile territory for including puzzles at every turn. This gave rise to the idea of placing hidden shrines throughout the open world—each requiring the player to solve problems of varying complexity—and, more generally, to the idea of providing an infinite number of ways to approach any conflict. For example, even the smallest enemy camp must be rigorously analyzed before the player launches an attack that can take an extremely wide variety of forms. Forcing players to deal not only with enemies, but also with the physical environment (landscape elements, weather, etc.), represents a completely new approach to gameplay in a *Zelda* game. The goal is to encourage players to try out different ideas in a process of trial and error, improving their skills by daring to try things that they're not even sure will actually work. For Fujibayashi, these fundamental elements have been there since the start of the series, but in different forms. The most important thing for him was to preserve the same sense of joy that players had found in the saga since its earliest beginnings.

Bit by bit, the director developed an increasingly detailed set of ideas about how he wanted to design the game. One important point from the *EDGE* interview was that progression in the game was intended to feel natural and intuitive for players from any culture and speakers of any language, so that everyone could feel the same satisfaction as they explored the game. Being able to chop down a tree so it falls across a ravine, thus allowing the player to cross it, is just one example of the type of logical situation that the team had to develop and refine at countless places throughout the game to make gameplay as intuitive as possible. As for the obvious desire to let players get lost in a vast natural world, it grew directly out of Fujibayashi's passion for the great outdoors. Although he no longer has much of a chance to express it in today's modern world, it was that spirit of adventure that guided Fujibayashi in the process of creating the game, just as it had guided Shigeru Miyamoto in developing the first *Zelda* game.

A TASTE OF TRUE FREEDOM

To learn how Hidemaro Fujibayashi went about convincing producer Eiji Aonuma and the father of the franchise, Shigeru Miyamoto, of the direction he had chosen to take, we can turn to an interview he gave to *Kotaku* on March 7, 2017. In the interview, he says that when he was asked what players would be able to do in this new *Zelda*, he answered: "You can do everything!" And to illustrate exactly what he meant, Fujibayashi presented his bosses with a version of the game in which the player could climb on any element of the scenery, with no specific objectives. Controller in hand, Shigeru Miyamoto then spent more than an hour climbing up and down trees, more fascinated by the possibilities of being able to climb anywhere he wanted than with the other challenges available in the demo! The director presents this moment as a major epiphany for him and his team about the rich potential inherent in this simple functionality, as they realized that it might have more to offer in terms of gameplay than a dungeon crawl or any other ordinary quest. As a result, the title quickly began to evolve toward the form as we know it today, setting aside the traditional approach to exploration in favor of a richer and more open-ended style of progression in which players can decide, at any moment, to climb the nearest mountain and take whatever shortcut they please. Fujibayashi added that this anecdote was also the starting point for the overall orientation of the gameplay system (which they called "multiplicative gameplay"), in which all the components of the environment can work together to create new and unexpected interactions. From that point on, instead of coming up with lots of individual new ideas, the development team tried to look at how each new situation could let players explore new ways to play.

Clearly, then, we mainly have director Hidemaro Fujibayashi to thank for the very open-ended orientation of *Breath of the Wild*, which arose directly from his passion for so-called "sandbox" games in which players can try out just about any interaction they like, with no real constraints. In the interview with *EDGE* magazine mentioned above, he explained that he had been strongly inspired by games like *Minecraft* and *Terraria* and their seemingly inexhaustible range of gameplay possibilities. Fascinated by these games and their unique approach of not imposing any specific objectives on players, but simply encouraging them to try out any idea they could possibly imagine, Fujibayashi began looking for ways to bring as much of this mindset as possible into *Breath of the Wild*. This explains why the finished game is so exciting in terms of its exploration aspect alone, intentionally leaving aside the series' usual structures.

DEVELOPMENT BEGINS

SHAKING THE FOUNDATIONS

The actual development process started in January 2013 with one guiding principle: the need to shake up the usual conventions of the series. Before getting underway, the *Breath of the Wild* team met to discuss which unchanging aspects of the saga they wanted to preserve at all costs. In his interview with *EDGE*, Fujibayashi explained: "We didn't want to change the basic nature of the *Zelda* games, we just wanted to change our approach to the series." So although their intent was to shake up the ancient foundations of the *Zelda* franchise, they certainly didn't want to damage its core essence along the way. As they thought about how *Breath of the Wild* could provide the same sense of discovery as the very first *Zelda* game, Fujibayashi realized that one of the original title's greatest strengths was its totally open-ended structure. Back in 1986, players had to discover where the next dungeon was and figure out a way to get there by themselves, with no explicit hints. A perfect approach for *Breath of the Wild*! The director also especially liked the idea of grounding the future of the series in its past roots. Right from the start of development, then, the team focused on preserving the sense of discovery that had defined the franchise since the beginning, by emphasizing exploration and puzzles and ensuring that players were consistently rewarded for every new secret they discovered. By combining all that with the idea of an open world, they established a clear overall direction for *Breath of the Wild* that was perfect for taking the series back to basics.

BACK TO BASICS

If there was one principle that seemed to guide the creative process for *The Legend of Zelda: Breath of the Wild*, it was the need to go back to the ideals of the original episode, released in 1986 on the Famicom Disk System in Japan, then in 1987 in the West as an NES cartridge (but not until October 1988 in France, according to an investigation by Florent Gorges in a special issue of the magazine *The Game: Les Cahiers de la Playhistoire Spécial Zelda*). Despite the machine's technical limitations, the vision of the first *Zelda*—as imagined by Shigeru Miyamoto and Takashi Tezuka, both completely unknown at the time— revealed its creators' ingenuity in achieving the impossible by offering what we can recognize today as a pioneering entry in the open world genre. But while we can now see it as a precursor to the impressive world of the 2017 episode, *The Legend of Zelda* was actually little more than a series of fixed screens, each representing a tiny slice of an environment that players had to explore by themselves. Arranged end-to-end like a life-size puzzle, this collection of individual screens formed the entire "overworld" area of the world of Hyrule; the game also included nine dungeon areas, each with its own map. Dropped into this completely open environment without the slightest indication of what they were expected to do, players were immediately confronted with choices that would define the very nature of their quest and make it totally unique; each quest was necessarily distinct from every other, defined by each player's choices at different branch points, guided by their own intuition.

One of *The Legend of Zelda*'s greatest strengths lay in its ability to let players lose themselves in the process of exploration—starting from the very first screen in the game, which sets the tone by allowing us to start out in any of four possible directions. Driven by the desire to learn what hides behind the cave entrance, which is the only element that really stands out in the starting area, players are soon rewarded for their curiosity with a wooden sword that will be essential for the adventure ahead. The inside of the cave is dark, illuminated only by two torches; inside, the player meets a mysterious old man whose entire life seems to have been leading up to the moment when he gives us this precious item—along with a warning about the dangers of the world outside. With that, the game's atmosphere has been established with just a few pixels, some brief dialogue, and the slightest hint of a story. The urge to start exploring is irresistible.

GOOD OLD-FASHIONED EXPLORATION

Much like the earliest tabletop role-playing games with their dungeons scribbled on scraps of graph paper, Miyamoto's creation reminds us of an era when players couldn't rely on a map or any other form of outside help to make their way through an adventure. Even a player with an excellent memory wouldn't have been foolish enough to set forth on their quest without taking careful notes on everything they discovered along the way, since even the slightest detail could be the key to making progress later on in the game. When we consider that any wall segment in the first *Zelda* game could be hiding the entrance to an underground passage or that a power bracelet allows Link to move gravestones aside, we can imagine how much time players spent on solving the game's mysteries one by one to improve their chances of making it through to the end. Similarly, although there were countless trees in the overworld, any one of them might also have secrets to reveal when set aflame with a candle bought for a handful of rupees from one of the rare merchants living in the hostile world of Hyrule. Those secrets could turn out to be lucrative rewards... or unexpected penalties, if a grumpy hermit decided to make Link pay for repairs to the front door he had just brutally smashed in! Despite its great simplicity and visual austerity, *The Legend of Zelda* managed to create an intriguing atmosphere—and more importantly, a real sense of freedom. These are essential qualities for any game focused on exploration and discovery. In today's era, when it seems impossible to imagine an RPG without a minimap and an icon marking the location of the next objective with uncanny accuracy, simply regaining the right to explore on one's own could be the saving grace for all those games that don't let us step off the straight and narrow path of the main story for even a second.

THE OPEN WORLD

Whether they were originally designed along these lines or not, nearly all of the biggest video game series have eventually taken a shot at the open world formula at some point in their evolution—with varying degrees of success. That's why, as unlikely as it might have seemed even a few years before, the idea of a *Zelda* game built on an open world design now seemed almost like the logical next step when seen as a way of returning to the ideals of the original game.

From very early in the process, Aonuma insisted on the importance of encouraging players to explore every corner of the world to discover what might be hidden behind this or that element of the environment. Using this approach, the landscape is no longer a mere backdrop that simply defines the limits of where we can go. Because he can now climb any mountainside and glide through the air with his "paraglider" (a sort of rudimentary parachute inspired by the Sailcloth in *Skyward Sword*), Link can continue his wanderings well beyond the horizon. A piece of artwork from *Breath of the Wild* drew a revealing parallel between an image of the new Link perched at the top of a high cliff, contemplating faraway vistas, and the same scene found among sketches made during the design phase for the first *Zelda* game. The apparent goal in both cases was to emphasize the immensity of the landscape around us—and above all, the player's ability to go wherever their curiosity leads them, with no restrictions whatsoever.

In the same spirit, the original Japanese version of the *Breath of the Wild* logo seems to be a nostalgic tip of the hat to the logo for the original *Zelda* game. In particular, the words *Zelda no Densetsu* (*The Legend of Zelda*) appear in almost exactly the same Japanese font as the one used for the original game on the Famicon Disk System (FDS). The subtitle *Breath of the Wild* appears a bit lower, under a line positioned in exactly the same way as the sword that appeared just under the title *Zelda no Densetsu* on the FDS episode. The similarities in terms of the logo's visual arrangement and spartan design are quite striking. As for the Western versions of *Breath of the Wild*, they opt for a logo much more similar to that of the episode *A Link to the Past*, with the Master Sword embedded in an identical way in the Z of the word *Zelda*. Looking closer at the Z, we can even see a mysterious little flower, which Eiji Aonuma referred to as a "Silent Princess" (*hime shizuka* in Japanese) in an "unboxing" video for the European limited edition of the game.

Having kept a close eye on the most relevant open world games to come out of the industry over the past few years, Eiji Aonuma made no secret of his interest for titles like *The Witcher 3*, *GTA* and *Skyrim* (especially with regard to the very distinct identities of the different cities in the latter game), which managed to stand out from the crowd without rejecting their origins. In the case of *Breath of the Wild*, the producer knew that the transition to an open world could be even riskier; above all, it was critical that his teams never lose sight of the elements that had always defined the essence of a *Zelda* game for longtime players. The feelings that players would experience with *Breath of the Wild* should never be incompatible with what they felt as they watched the hero's progression in other episodes of the series. And even if this new evolution of the series had a different look and feel, it should still be a journey of initiation at its core, in which Link discovers for himself the tools he needs to keep driving his quest forward. As long as those promises were kept, the title seemed to have an excellent chance to stand out from the crowd with its emphasis on harmony with nature, combining the melancholy of *Shadow of the Colossus* with the poetry of a game like *Shenmue* set in the breathtaking landscapes of Guilin.

But the challenge was a sizable one: if the team was unable to balance and fill out this vast open world and give players a plausible reason for every action they were asked to perform, *Breath of the Wild*'s open world could end up feeling more repetitive than revolutionary. To avoid this pitfall, Fujibayashi not only emphasized the omnipresence of collectible resources throughout the environment, but also spoke of more innovative concepts like the need to change clothes regularly to adapt to changing weather conditions. In the interview with *EDGE* magazine, he also explained his intent to develop more crafting options (allowing players to upgrade their equipment themselves through the use of various materials), going beyond the handful of possibilities available in *Skyward Sword*. In *Breath of the Wild*, players should be able to draw on a wide variety of resources to cook up all sorts of different dishes, each providing its own unique bonuses. As such, each player can prepare for the adventure in their own way, whether that means stockpiling healing items, emphasizing weapon upgrades, or even leaving the whole crafting component aside to rely on their combat skills alone. The ultimate goal was to compensate for the disappearance of certain older core elements of the franchise, like the little hearts that could be found just by cutting herbs, with new gameplay routines as intuitive as the need to hunt in order to feed oneself and recover health.

As for the physical size of the open world, it was the result of long deliberations about how large the playable area should be in order to give players a sense of getting lost in a real environment without discouraging them from exploring every corner of it. In the end, the team decided on an area about the same size as the city of Kyoto, the director's home town and the location of Nintendo headquarters. At twelve times the size of the world of *Twilight Princess*, it was important that the distances between locations in this open world feel natural, whether exploring it on foot or on horseback. It would also need to contain a substantial number of different points of interest—and basing the world size on Kyoto was a good choice here, since the city is filled with tourist locations, which served as sources of inspiration for Fujibayashi and his team as they decided how to distribute key locations around the world.

AMAZING DESIGN PROTOTYPES

Following Aonuma's decision to rethink the basic conventions of the series, the internal forum for Nintendo's development teams was quickly inundated with all sorts of suggestions from team members. Everyone presented their ideas, even some that were a bit outlandish or unrealistic, in hopes of surprising and entertaining players in all kinds of new ways. This process led to some truly amazing design prototypes, which were revealed to the public on March 1, 2017, just two days before the title finally appeared in stores. Nintendo chose the Game Developers Conference (GDC), a key industry event held in San Francisco, to share some of the secrets of *Breath of the Wild*'s design. For director Hidemaro Fujibayashi, it was a perfect occasion to talk about his team's development process. His conference session, entitled "Change and Constant: Breaking Conventions with *The Legend of Zelda: Breath of the Wild*," focused on the idea of breaking the series' conventions while preserving its original spirit.

THE OLD-SCHOOL PROTOTYPE FOR BREATH OF THE WILD

Fujibayashi began by reaffirming the project's guiding principle: the importance of turning *Breath of the Wild* into the culmination of the ideals behind the original 1986 *Zelda*. And the best way to illustrate this idea was to show a video featuring images from a 2D prototype designed by *Breath of the Wild* technical director Takuhiro Dohta. Used briefly at the very start of development, this retro prototype borrowed the 8-bit style of *The Legend of Zelda* to test out the gameplay mechanics of *Breath of the Wild*. Clearly, the objective was to give the GDC audience a concrete sense of what producer Eiji Aonuma had been talking about since the start of the project: a return to the series' roots. In the sequence presented in the video, the world is visually identical to that of the original *Zelda*, but it is no longer subdivided into fixed screens arranged one after another. Instead, the player can wander freely through its different environments, which could be seen as a schematic representation of the ones planned for *Breath of the Wild*.

During the session, Fujibayashi emphasized that this experimental combination based on 2D graphics allowed the development team to evaluate the viability of different interactions with the open world that were being considered for the new game. The goal was to ensure that all of the player's actions would have repercussions on both the environment and the creatures living in it—a playful way for the team to directly visualize which gameplay mechanics worked well and which ones would need to be changed. For example, the video showed the 8-bit Link shooting an arrow through a campfire to ignite the forest on the other side, then pushing the logs into the water using a tree leaf. None of this was possible in the first *Zelda* game, but it would be in *Breath of the Wild*.

The idea was also to emphasize the team's intention to tear down the barriers that had limited players' freedom of exploration and the possibilities offered by the new *Zelda* to go well beyond what players can do in a typical open world game. The video then presented the same scene as it appeared in *Breath of the Wild*—with a much more realistic look, to be sure, but still with the same sense of "playing" with the world around us. If the player's progress is blocked by a deep chasm, it's up to them to think of taking out their ax to chop down a tree and use it as a makeshift bridge. It should be possible to resolve any problematic situation in a number of different ways, depending on each individual player's thought process. Above all, seeing this kind of trick presented in a game with modern graphics, side-by-side with an archaic-looking prototype based on an almost prehistoric era of video game development, was enough to bring a thrill of excitement to anyone who had been following the medium since the 1980s.

But of course, the transition to the 3D environments of *Breath of the Wild* was far from an easy one—especially when considering the use of different terrain types, which required the team to reconsider the time needed to get from one point to another on the map. An area that the player could get through in a few seconds in 2D could take quite a bit longer when crossing rough or mountainous terrain. As a result, the development team had to deal with a certain number of constraints to come up with a 3D implementation of the ideas suggested by the retro prototype and to ensure that the placement of the various points of interest was appropriate for a three-dimensional world map. That's why all of the different elements in the game were placed as the world was being built, with travel times carefully calculated to avoid breaking the rhythm of the game.

Hidemaro Fujibayashi added that by keeping in mind an image of the first *Zelda* game, in which the player was confronted with new puzzles to solve in each new screen, the *Breath of the Wild* development team was able to maintain a consistent focus on keeping players astonished and amazed at every turn. Besides its role in the development process, the retro prototype also made a big impression on the public, and Internet commenters began dreaming of one day playing an old-school version of *Breath of the Wild*...

ABANDONED EXPERIMENTS

Besides this nostalgic tribute to the first *Zelda* game, the conference session also revealed other fascinating steps in the creative process that led to *Breath of the Wild*, during which a number of unusual ideas were tested but ultimately abandoned. For example, artistic director Satoru Takizawa presented a series of design sketches relating to prototypes called *Hyrule Wars* and *The Legend of Zelda: Invasion*, which took a more futuristic and warlike approach than the final game. In *Invasion*, we see Link watching the arrival of a giant flying saucer as it prepares to fire a missile salvo at his planet—an image that might seem completely out of sync with the spirit of the series if we hadn't already experienced an alien invasion in a well-known scene from *Majora's Mask*. You may recall a long night spent with the hero of that Nintendo 64 episode trying to stop aliens from closing in on a farm and kidnapping its... cows?! But does that mean that absolutely anything goes in a *Zelda* game? Not necessarily, even though that scene is inarguably one of the funniest moments in the entire series.

In any case, sketches like these showed how willing the development teams were to experiment in all kinds of daring and unexpected ways. As if to hammer the point home, the last few illustrations revealed in this conference session imagined Link as a modern biker, a cosmonaut, and a guitarist in full rock regalia! From the retro tribute to these fantastic and improbable visions, designing *Breath of the Wild* had clearly given its creators a chance to let their imaginations run wild.

A HIGH-STAKES ANNOUNCEMENT

Although the first hints that development was starting on a new *Zelda* game for the Wii U had trickled out at the 2011 edition of E3 (the Electronic Entertainment Expo) in Los Angeles, it wasn't until 2014 that the game was officially announced. But it's important to keep in mind that during that same period, Nintendo was already actively working on two other installments in the franchise: the 3DS episode *A Link Between Worlds* and the high-definition remastered version of *The Wind Waker* for the Wii U. So it was really on June 10, 2014, at the 20th edition of E3, that Eiji Aonuma announced (without mentioning its full name) that the next *Zelda* game would come out on the Wii U in 2015. Opting once again for a prerecorded video released via Nintendo Direct, the producer began by mentioning the difficulties his teams had encountered in trying to effectively convey a sense of exploring a vast open world since the advent of 3D graphics. Taking the fragmented structure of *The Wind Waker*'s ocean-based world as an example, Aonuma explained his initial intention to find ways to restore a greater sense of cohesion and offer players a huge world that would really feel like a unified whole.

Laying out the issue in this way provided a perfect transition to the first images of the next *Zelda* game, which then appeared on the screen. Immense and lush, the environment spreads out as far as the eye can see, like an ode to the beauty of nature. Swept by the wind and the shadows of clouds far overhead, the grass waves gently in the foreground as a silhouette appears in the distance: a hooded rider sitting quietly on his horse. What Eiji Aonuma was promising with this image was a world without limits for players to explore, free of all the usual restrictions. In short, a truly open world—something that the series had never tried before, except in the very first game with its groundbreaking world of one hundred and twenty-eight screens forming the first region of the kingdom of Hyrule. The creator then asked viewers to imagine being able to wander wherever they liked in those wide-open spaces, with no obligation to follow a predefined sequence of objectives. Aonuma concluded this first glimpse of the new *Zelda* game with a demonstration that this land was not always as peaceful as it seemed and that dangerous enemies could emerge to threaten our hero at any moment. A sudden noise shatters the quiet atmosphere and replaces it with a sharp twinge of panic. The birds fly away in a rush, the horse whinnies and rears up, and Link struggles to get his steed under control as a threatening creature comes into view behind him. Racing toward him at a shocking speed and firing a ray that destroys whatever it touches, the multi-legged monster scuttles along after our hero, who dodges, then flees at a full gallop toward a makeshift bridge that is smashed to splinters before his eyes by the vicious attacker. The close-up that follows gives viewers a clear look at the game's new art direction, reminiscent of Japanese animation, as Link pulls back his hood to reveal a new look, proudly showing off his blue tunic and blond ponytail. The video ends on a breathtaking high note as Link draws his bow to fire an explosive arrow right into the creature's eye, then leaps into the air to finish off his enemy in a thrilling slow-motion shot. Finally, "2015" appears on the screen, promising an imminent release for the new episode that now officially had everyone's attention.

A flood of questions followed the announcement, and Nintendo's sometimes vague responses led to all kinds of wild rumors. For example, the fact that Eiji Aonuma did not explicitly confirm right away that the main character was Link had people wondering for a while whether they would be playing as a completely new character—maybe even as a woman. After all, *Hyrule Warriors Legends* had already explored this possibility, introducing a female alter ego for the first time in the series—a Cucco farmer named Linkle who knew her way around a crossbow. Given the open world design of the new game, it also made sense that players might be able to design their own avatar. But the producer himself denied these rumors fairly quickly.

In any case, it seemed that there was still an enormous amount of work to be done, and questions were immediately raised about Nintendo's ability to stick to the 2015 release date when so few specific elements had been revealed up to that point. So the team dived back into the development process with more energy than ever—and entered a period of radio silence that would last for almost two years.

NINTENDO'S MESSAGE

Kept carefully hidden until the summer of 2014, the face of *The Legend of Zelda: Breath of the Wild* didn't fully emerge until E3 2016. As the convention got under way in June of that year, the only widely-seen images of the game were from that wild ride in which Link had battled with a mysterious mechanical creature. Although we didn't know it at the time, that creature was one of the Guardians that would be the focus of one part of the game's story. Hoping to make a big splash at the US event by breaking its long months of silence, Nintendo chose this occasion to reveal a new trailer with a decidedly poetic feel, emphasizing the sense of adventure that would be the focus of this new *Zelda* game. From a PR perspective, the reasons for the publisher's decision were clear: the Japanese giant wanted to focus all the attention on this one playable title, since none of Nintendo's other games had playable prototypes available at the time. The focus on the new *Zelda* also included an extravagant booth that soon became the number one attraction for everyone attending E3 2016. It seemed that no one could bear to leave the convention without spending a few minutes checking out the game that had been such a mystery until then.

THE FIRST REAL IMAGES OF THE PROJECT

Needless to say, the trailer revealed at E3 2016 quickly made its way around the world, since it was the first time the public was able to see certain concrete elements of the gameplay and narrative setting of the new *Zelda* game. Skillfully orchestrated by Nintendo, the communication process that had been on standby for so long as it waited for the project to progress suddenly leapt into motion as the game's impending release became a reality. For everyone who saw the new video, its core message was a promise of total freedom that would go beyond anything they had ever seen in a video game. But Nintendo would still have to prove that the aspects of the new *Zelda* that had been revealed up to that point would be sufficiently well-achieved to convince a skeptical gaming public.

The E3 2016 trailer opens with the words of a young woman who does not appear on screen, but whose identity most viewers were able to guess, telling us to "open your eyes" to the majestic panorama laid out before us. An impressive array of wild environments appears on the screen in the three-minute video, imparting a sense of solitude in which the viewer's intrusive gaze seems like the only thing that might disrupt the harmony of nature. The wide variety of landscapes (plains, canyons, coastlines, mountains, forests, a ruined temple) hints at a vast world much grander than anything the series has had to offer in the past—and above all, much more alive. For while the video is striking for its lack of human beings, other animals are plentiful in this world that seems to exist in another time. Ducks paddle on a sunlit lake, deer frolic in the woods, ibis take flight in a desert canyon... and, in an unexpected twist, the silhouette of a giant skeleton lumbers along a distant ridge as lightning splits the night sky above a shattered Guardian, invoking a sense of looming danger. This time, the woman's voice addresses Link directly (*"Open your eyes! Wake up, Link!"*), attempting to awaken the hero that the kingdom so desperately needs. The trailer then takes a more epic turn as the hero leaps from a high cliff and deploys his paraglider to soar over the vast wilderness below.

In less than a minute, Nintendo gave viewers a clear illustration of how the new *Zelda* intends to once again make freedom of exploration its top priority. Not only do the landscapes seem to form a unified whole, but viewers are also excited at the idea of being able to use the paraglider to travel wherever they like in the world. The rest of the video shows even more explicitly how players

will have to adapt to their environment—by taming the animals they meet there, for example. Hiding in the high grass, Link creeps up on a group of wild horses, then leaps onto one of them, holding on tight as it whinnies and bucks. Given the huge impact that Link's mare Epona had on exploration in *Ocarina of Time*, the idea of exploring the vast environments seen here on horseback was bound to get *Zelda* fans excited. Later in the trailer, we see the steed and its rider galloping over an endless stone bridge, followed by several shots of the new Link's everyday activities. In short, the game is not only about wandering the natural world to discover its secrets; players will also have to think about how to come to grips with the physical environment in each location. Hunting and fishing are no longer mere leisure activities, but essential tools for survival, providing the basic ingredients for a variety of dishes whipped up by our hero in a pot or two over the campfire.

Returning to the series' origins in pure fantasy, this video of the new *Zelda* also revealed what would turn out to be the most important tool in this new episode: the Sheikah Slate. Marked with the eye symbol that had been used since *Ocarina of Time* to represent the tribe that protects Hyrule's royal family, this item would be the key to solving the various puzzles that Link will encounter throughout the game. Functioning as both a high-powered magnet and an ice block generator on liquid surfaces, the slate offers a whole range of new possibilities that would be illustrated in greater detail in later videos from Nintendo. But the focus in this trailer remained centered on combat, reassuring fans with a montage of action sequences that show off Link's agility as he shifts seamlessly from dodges to counterattacks—as well as the wide variety of weapons he can steal from his enemies to use against them. Along the same lines, seeing Link in plate mail armor or fur-lined clothes introduced the exciting new possibility of equipping our hero with all kinds of different gear, not just the handful of tunics he typically wore in other games in the series. On this point, as with the choice of available weapons, Nintendo freely acknowledged that *Breath of the Wild* had borrowed a certain number of ideas from Western RPGs and open world games—ideas that one wouldn't necessarily have expected to find in a *Zelda* game. But this first glimpse of the game suggested a real desire to explore new directions. If nothing else, the combination of all these new elements certainly piqued the public's curiosity.

The story, meanwhile, remained a closely guarded secret, even as certain fans began to propose all sorts of wild theories, including thoughts about how the new game fit into the overall timeline of the series. The trailer's closing image had shown the legendary Master Sword resting chipped and moss-covered on its pedestal, having clearly suffered the ravages of time as it waited patiently for the return of the chosen one. It's that same sword that pierces the Z of the word *Zelda* in the game's logo; a tiny flower sprouting from the bottom of the logo eloquently represents the importance of nature in *Breath of the Wild* and stands as a symbol for the new episode as a whole. We will analyze this point in more detail later on, but for now, let us simply note Nintendo's desire to reach out to longtime fans and reassure them that the open world aspect would not be the only exciting part of the new game; it would also provide its fair share of story developments relating to key elements of the franchise.

A NARROW FOCUS ON THE OPEN WORLD

Between the E3 convention in June 2016 and the game's release date—which would ultimately be postponed to March 3, 2017—Nintendo's communications relating to *Breath of the Wild* focused almost exclusively on the open world dimension of the new adventure. This choice can be explained by Nintendo's concern with maintaining as much secrecy as possible about the game's narrative aspects, but also by its desire to raise players' awareness of everything the title would have to offer in terms of freedom of exploration. For example, a number of demo sessions presented to the press highlighted the immense size of the new regions of Hyrule, dropping players into the game with no clear indication of what to do in areas that seemed almost too vast to fully explore, even though they represented only a tiny portion of the world. After all, Aonuma had announced that the map would cover an area the size of Kyoto—almost 320 square miles! What Nintendo wanted to show was that players would be able to explore this world in any way they chose, far from any concern with the game's main storyline. The adventure would also be radically different for each player, since everyone would have a different experience based on the specific places they chose to visit and the specific actions they took there.

Alongside the initial message of total freedom, Nintendo had now added a line of communication based more around changes to the series, comparable to the approach taken by other well-known franchises that had opted for a reboot: *Tomb Raider, DmC: Devil May Cry, Alone in the Dark*, and *Castlevania: Lords of Shadow*, to name just a few. And yet Nintendo had never presented *Breath of the Wild* as a reboot. Still, it's not hard to imagine that the team could have easily gone in that direction if they hadn't opted to develop a totally original story for the new installment.

In the final stretch before the game's release, communications around *Breath of the Wild* placed a greater emphasis on the realistic representation of the day/night cycle and changing weather conditions in the open world. A twenty-three-minute time lapse video was the clearest example of this approach. Throughout the entire sequence, which unfolds in real time and shows the passage of an entire in-game day from a single fixed perspective, we see Link contemplating the distant landscape from a high cliff without showing the slightest sign of fatigue... In another video, we see our hero in fine form, surfing down snowy slopes on his shield like a snowboarder—and showing off his archery skills to boot, in a nod to Legolas, the elf immortalized in Peter Jackson's *Lord of the Rings* trilogy.

Finally, the last category of trailers released by Nintendo in the run-up to March 3rd was mainly concerned with bonuses included with the special edition of the game and with presenting a number of new amiibo figurines that had been announced for the game's release. Designed by Nintendo, amiibos could be recognized by the company's more recent consoles to unlock various in-game bonuses. For the new *Zelda* game, for example, a trailer announced that the Wolf Link amiibo designed for the HD edition of *Twilight Princess* could be used with *Breath of the Wild* to make a wolf companion appear in-game. This was more than a simple gimmick, since the animal actively helps Link in his journey by warning him of nearby enemies or going out to hunt for food. On the other hand, no details were provided about the effects provided by the other amiibos created specifically to accompany the new game—and as it turned out, their role was simply to generate a few rare items and various types of bonuses (weapons, food, etc.) to help the player progress more easily. Although these figurines were hardly essential to the game, there's no denying that this marketing approach paid off by helping to ratchet up the excitement just a few weeks before the game was to come out.

By putting its full weight behind the new *Zelda* game in a range of carefully targeted presentations highlighting the vast potential of its ambitious open world design, in the space of a few months Nintendo managed to convince the press and the gaming public that the release of *Breath of the Wild* might well be the biggest event of 2017. All eyes then turned to the Web, where wild new theories and rumors emerged every day about what was sure to be a totally new kind of *Zelda* game.

Still, although we can hardly accuse Eiji Aonuma and his teams of not communicating actively about the gameplay and the general orientation of the new *Zelda* game in the long months between E3 2016 and the game's ultimate release date, there was one point that was almost never discussed: the game's narrative background. Here again, the absence of any specific information about the game's story or characters was clearly part of an overall strategy on the publisher's part to draw players into a fascinating world without revealing any of the mysteries around its storyline. As if to reassure those who might be concerned, brief images of characters from the various well-known tribes of the *Zelda* universe (Zoras, Gorons, Ritos) eventually made their way into the lengthy trailer released on January 13, 2017—the only one that ever bothered to address the issue.

It seemed that not a day went by without a new piece of *Zelda* news lighting up the Internet, and the publisher took care to make its own contribution to the discussion as well. On March 14, Nintendo released three "making of" videos featuring interviews with members of the development team, to provide a behind-the-scenes look at the development process. The first video looked at the challenges the team faced as the project was getting started in January 2013 and went over a few experimental concepts that were not included in the final version, as we'll see in more detail in the next section. The second video focused on how the open world experience was transposed to the *Zelda* franchise and on the combat system and the innovative ways in which it interacts with the physics engine to revolutionize the way Link's fights would unfold. Finally, the third "making-of" video explained the need to reinvent the series' most popular characters and convey the story in a new way, to go along with the new orientation taken by the game. On a side note, the video also revealed that at a certain stage of the project, the team had considered including a tiny town of tiny people in which Link would shrink down to the same size as in the episode *The Legend of Zelda: The Minish Cap* for the GBA—but in the end, it was not to be.

DELAYS

According to Shigeru Miyamoto, the development of *Breath of the Wild*—the full name of which was finally revealed at E3 2016—represented over four years of hard work by a team of no less than 300 people. That made it Nintendo's most ambitious project ever—and to ensure that it would be a success, the company enlisted the help of Monolith Soft, a studio known for its experience with open world RPGs like *Xenoblade Chronicles* for the Wii and *Xenoblade Chronicles X* for the Wii U. In all, about 100 developers who had worked on *Xenoblade Chronicles* wound up collaborating closely with Nintendo staff, sharing their knowhow with Eiji Aonuma's team for everything relating to the structure of the open world. With support from level designers who were used to working with wide-open spaces, Nintendo was able to design an open world that was physically structured to ensure a balanced experience, even as a whole team of designers each made their own contributions to it. To avoid any inconsistencies that might arise from this profusion of ideas, director Hidemaro Fujibayashi set up a system in which each developer could test the consequences of their work on other aspects of the game. Each time a milestone was reached, all the different specialized teams (programmers, designers, artists, composers, etc.) would stop and simply play the game for a while, sometimes for more than a week straight, to make sure that one group's progress wasn't hurting the efforts of the other groups. Although this way of working might seem very time-consuming, Fujibayashi explained that in fact, it helped to reduce overall development time by ensuring that everything was in perfect order before proceeding to the next stage. By giving everyone a chance to get a hands-on sense of what their colleagues were working on, this form of horizontal and collaborative communication tore down the usual barriers between different specializations, preventing key information from becoming isolated within this or that group.

In a message published on social media, Takuhiro Dohta, the technical director on *Breath of the Wild*, also mentioned the importance of the debugging phase, in response to questions about the astoundingly small number of bugs for such an enormous game. Dohta explained that, unlike most open world games, *Breath of the Wild* had been designed by first establishing the rules that would govern and thereby stabilize the world, rather than filling the world with various preconceived elements—and that this approach had prevented many bugs from arising in the first place. Another useful trick had been to create scripts that let the game run by itself in order to immediately flag new bugs by way of email alerts. But the most important tool to help the team make all the necessary fixes in the debugging phase was a playtesting tool that allowed them to gather all the relevant information about each playtesting session in a centralized location in real time. By tracking where players died, how many hearts they had at different points throughout the game, and analyzing their movements around the map, the tool played an essential role in balancing the overall difficulty of the game. That's not to say that the team felt the need to make the game less challenging—quite the opposite, in fact. For example, when Fujibayashi learned that most players were dying by accidentally falling from towers, he preferred to leave the climbing difficulty alone, encouraging players to learn from their mistakes and be more careful on later attempts. In an interview with the US site *The Verge*, the director also mentioned that allowing players to get lost in the vast expanses of the in-game world was a conscious decision that the game design team had intentionally chosen to emphasize. In the end, it was this set of homemade tools that allowed Nintendo to provide a level of quality control that was fairly incredible for a game of this size.

But the game's scheduled release date, originally set for 2015, soon proved impossible to meet, and in March of that year, Aonuma decided to give the development teams more time to complete their mission. Nintendo also took advantage of this extra time to localize the game into eight different languages, making it accessible to a wider range of players around the world. So it's not surprising that E3 2015 didn't feature any updates on the new *Zelda* game—or that the subject was practically taboo until the following April, when Nintendo announced that the game's release would be postponed until 2017. The delay was also due in part to the arrival of the Switch, Nintendo's new console (originally known by the code name NX), which meant that the teams in charge of thc ncxt *Zelda* gamc would have to develop an additional version for that platform as well. An increasing number of trailers were released in 2016, finally giving fans a concrete look at the enticing promises of an episode that aimed to shake up all the most basic conventions of the series. In the end, the title would not be a Wii U exclusive and would instead enjoy a simultaneous release on both consoles on March 3, 2017—the same day that the Switch itself was set to launch. This choice obviously echoed a similar decision for the release of *Twilight Princess* on GameCube and Wii, a point that we will return to later in our analysis.

FIRST REACTIONS

Nintendo's communications teams chose to reveal little or nothing about the content of *The Legend of Zelda: Breath of the Wild* before its worldwide release, well aware that the quality of the title would depend on a successful launch for its new Switch console. Given the circumstances, it would be impossible to dissociate *Zelda* from this new hybrid console, which could either plug into a TV screen or be played on the go like a handheld console. And right up until March 3, 2017, communications about both products were closely intertwined in an avalanche of ads highlighting the console's extreme flexibility. For Nintendo, the days of having to change our daily routines to incorporate gaming time were over. From now on, technology would have to adapt to our lifestyles, not the other way around. And because the Switch could so easily transform from a home console to a handheld console, it would meet these new requirements perfectly.

UNANIMOUS CRITICAL PRAISE

Nevertheless, on the eve of the console launch, its success was anything but assured, as most players were not yet convinced of the hybrid concept and weren't sure they would be able to make full use of it in their daily lives. On the other hand, the aura of greatness around *Breath of the Wild*, as the Nintendo Switch launch title, had generated massive interest among Nintendo and *Zelda* fans for the game's release. Just days before the game came out, critics turned up the pressure another notch by rewarding the new *Zelda* game with glowing reviews and eye-popping scores. On the *Metacritic* site, which calculates average review scores for movie, music, and game releases, *Breath of the Wild* for the Switch had an average score of 97% across ninety-one different reviews. An exceptional score that few titles have ever surpassed—though still not enough to beat the 99% score earned by *Ocarina of Time*, the masterpiece that many fans consider to be the best *Zelda* game of all time.

The public quickly realized that something unexpected was happening, and the few remaining skeptics took a second look at the game everyone was rushing to praise. Needless to say, Nintendo immediately launched an even more intense round of marketing communications based on these review scores, releasing an ad that highlighted no fewer than eight magazines and websites that had given the game their top score (*IGN, Polygon, EDGE, Gamespot, Time, Giant Bomb, Forbes,* and *Game Informer*) and two others that gave it "only" 9/10 (the French sites *Gamekult* and *Gameblog*). A seemingly endless list of critics from websites and print media around the world gave the game their best possible scores (*Famitsu, NintendoLife, Destructoid, The Game, Jeux Vidéo Magazine*)—including some that normally make a point of never awarding perfect scores, even for their favorite games. The French site *Jeuxvideo.com* provides an especially clear example: after an unprecedented controversy over the 20/20 score it had awarded to *The Wind Waker*, with equal numbers of commenters defending it and denouncing it, the editors had imposed a de facto ban on perfect review scores for video games. Against that backdrop, the site's 20/20 score for *Breath of the Wild* was filled with symbolic value, and the editors even went so far as to organize a 7-hour *Let's Play Live* and publish an editorial explaining their "unapologetic review." The article described the game as "an event unique enough to be seen as an outlier by our readers, who haven't experienced anything like it on the pages of *Jeuxvideo.com* in the past 14 years." The main point was to remove the untouchable aura from the 20/20 score, too often perceived as a taboo, as long as the game that received it was truly worthy of a place in the video game pantheon.

While critics regularly pointed out certain technical imperfections in the game, virtually all of the reviews published when *Breath of the Wild* came out were overflowing with praise for the game's ability to immerse players in its unique world. For *Gamekult*, "this new *Zelda* game shakes up many of the saga's conventions and improves upon them, without forgetting or betraying its legendary history, and finally gives players complete control of the adventure."

At *Gamergen*, we read that "the more hours we spend with the game, the more we fall under its spell, and the less we notice its faults; in other words, we're falling in love." Then this: "*Breath of the Wild* is a worthy representative of a franchise that dares to question its oldest habits." For *Gameblog*, "*Breath of the Wild* is a quiet but passionate love letter to the series, subtly blending the best elements of each previous installment." The author adds that "while this *Zelda* does have its faults, they are easy to forget when a game is this generous and this revolutionary for a series which, for all its great qualities, had been resting on its laurels for many years." *Extralife* argues that "this episode is a stylish realization of the original vision that we first glimpsed in the original *Zelda* game thirty years ago [...] It goes back to the series' original values by inviting us to create our own story and complete our own quest in whatever way best fits our personal style." But what impact would such a radical change have on the overall image of the series? According to the editors of *JeuxActu*, "*Breath of the Wild* is one of the most beautiful experiences we've ever had the honor to enjoy. A masterpiece of rare perfection that skillfully surpasses the technical constraints of its platform to offer an adventure that leaves us forever changed." *Le Journal du Geek*, meanwhile, offers the bold headline "*Zelda* is dead and Nintendo killed it," highlighting *Breath of the Wild*'s fateful decision to finally push the series outside of its comfort zone and shake up its long-standing conventions. "After twenty-one years, Nintendo has finally exorcised the ghost of *Ocarina of Time*. What an incredible thrill." In reading these passionate words about *Breath of the Wild*, it's hard to resist sharing the reviewers' enthusiasm over the incredible wealth of experiences the game has to offer in well over a hundred hours of play!

IMPRESSIVE SALES

Would the Switch have had a successful launch without *Zelda* as its standard-bearer? It seems doubtful at best. In every part of the world, the vast majority of consumers who bought the console on day one chose *Breath of the Wild* as their only game, and many of them picked up the console specifically in order to play the new *Zelda* episode. Of course, the initial lineup for the Nintendo Switch didn't include that many interesting games—other than this infinitely promising title that the Web had been gushing about for months. It seems safe to assume that the aura around the new *Zelda* game is what made the launch of this new hybrid console a success. In Japan, *Famitsu* magazine notes that just 3 days after it came out, the Nintendo Switch had already sold 330,637 units. A thoroughly impressive figure, beating comparable numbers for the Wii U and the PS4, but still short of Nintendo's best all-time console launches for the Game Boy Advance (over 600,000 units!), the Nintendo DS, the Wii, and the 3DS. Meanwhile, in an interview with the *New York Times*, Nintendo of America president Reggie Fils-Aimé was already boasting of a North American record. During the first forty-eight hours, Switch sales in the US had already surpassed those of any other Nintendo console—and things were looking even better in Europe. In France, for example, the Switch sold 105,000 units in its first three days, putting the new hybrid console ahead of all its direct and indirect competitors; neither the Wii nor the PS4 had sold equivalent numbers there.

Clearly, the success of the Switch launch went hand in hand with the success of *Breath of the Wild*, which became Nintendo's biggest launch title ever in Europe, Australia, and New Zealand—even beating out *Wii Sports*, which was bundled with the Wii when it first came out. The game sold 193,000 copies in Japan the first week (for the Switch and Wii U), 130,000 in Europe (including 96,000 for the Switch), and 1.34 million worldwide by March 14, 2017, with Nintendo hoping to break the 2 million mark by March 2018. These results were all the more impressive considering that the title was not included in any bundles; consumers had to buy it separately from the console. But despite this limitation, *Breath of Wild* sold even better than the legendary *Super Mario 64* in North America! While these figures are nothing truly exceptional for an episode of the *Zelda* franchise, it's interesting to note the extent to which this warm reception had defied everyone's predictions. And while Nintendo stock had lost 5.75% of its value within a few hours of the company's official presentation of the Switch on January 13, 2017, it gained 6% from March 3-6, 2017, when the console arrived in stores.

In late March 2017, the NPD Group analytics firm evaluated the Switch's US launch as "Nintendo's best hardware launch and the second-best launch for any platform since 1995, the year when NPD began tracking this category." Over the same period, the only game to outsell *Breath of the Wild* in the United States was *Ghost Recon: Wildlands*, but the Nintendo title still sold an impressive 900,000 copies in the US. Worldwide, a total of 2.74 million Switch consoles were sold in the first month after its launch, and by June 25, 2017, the Switch had sold 1 million units in Japan alone despite shortages in many locations. The console's strong performance was driven in large part by exceptional sales for *Mario Kart 8 Deluxe* in Japan (501,614 copies sold), according to figures reported by the Japanese magazine *Famitsu*. A remake of a Wii U title, it even managed to steal the top spot from *Breath of the Wild* with its 460,480 copies sold in Japan, despite a later release date (April 28). In an interview with the *Gamekult* website on June 15, 2017, Philippe Lavoué, the managing director of Nintendo France, said he "expects to achieve an installed base of 1 million consoles in the first twelve months of operation" in France and described the initial sales of *Mario Kart 8 Deluxe* as "stratospheric"!

Expansion Pass or wet blanket?

On February 14, 2017, producer Eiji Aonuma appeared in a new video to announce the release of an "Expansion Pass" for *Breath of the Wild*—in other words, extensions to the game in the form of paid downloadable content. While this approach is quite common in the video game industry, Nintendo is not usually in the habit of exploiting this marketing technique to make extra money from its most committed players. Looking back, many players will fondly recall the DLC offered for *Mario Kart 8*, *Hyrule Warriors* and *Super Smash Bros.* (on Wii U and 3DS), which were relatively well-received by the community because they provided a real added value. On the other hand, the excessive number and exorbitant price of the DLCs for *Fire Emblem Awakening* on the 3DS had faced harsh criticism in light of the fact that the DLC could easily wind up costing more than the original game. Given this history, the announcement of an expansion pass for *Breath of the Wild* immediately raised concerns among critics and fans about how frequently Nintendo might resort to paid DLC for games like *Zelda* too.

Even more problematic was the fact that the Expansion Pass in question was made up of two separate packs that could not be bought separately from one another. This was the part of the announcement that proved most controversial, leaving fans feeling angry and betrayed by Nintendo's apparent refusal to let them choose which content they wanted to buy. Specifically, they would have to pay a whopping $25 for the full range of content Aonuma had announced—and too bad for them if they were only really interested in one of the two packs. This approach was seen as unfair by the vast majority of fans, for whom only a whole new narrative chapter could truly be considered essential; the other bonuses offered were not necessarily worth the high price.

In addition, the different packs that made up this Expansion Pass were to be released over a period of several months, with the last one set for release at the end of 2017. In other words, buying the Expansion Pass when the game first came out would only give players access to a few fairly meager bonuses (three chests, one of which contained a outfit with the Switch logo), after which they would have to wait until June 30 to get the first DLC truly worthy of the name with the so-called "Master Trials" pack. Even then, the new content was limited to a few special survival-type challenges ("The Trial of the Sword") and a new, higher difficulty level, along with an option that highlights where Link has been on the map and a handful of special outfits (including a mask that vibrates whenever Koroks are nearby). The one good idea here resides in the fact that acquiring these costumes also unlocks new optional quests. But only the final pack, scheduled for the end of 2017 and entitled "The Champions' Ballad," was really of much interest to players, who were curious to explore a mysterious new chapter in the story and the new dungeon that came with it.

Of course, the Expansion Pass was made available for both the Switch and Wii U versions of the game, and there's no reason to assume that Nintendo won't stir controversy again with later releases of the same type. According to Bill Trinen, Senior Product Marketing Manager at Nintendo of America, in comments reported on *IGN*, this content was not material that had been cut from the original game, but truly new content added after the fact for the sole purpose of extending players' time with the game. While players are right to be skeptical, we can certainly understand that the creators of a world as rich as the one in *Breath of the Wild* would want to get as much mileage out of it as they could, especially if doing so would allow players who had already finished the adventure to return to it again.

ZELDA

THE HISTORY OF A LEGENDARY SAGA
VOLUME 2: BREATH OF THE WILD

CHAPTER II

UNIVERSE

EYOND the fascinating story of its creation, *The Legend of Zelda: Breath of the Wild* had also earned a spot among the most intriguing episodes of the series even before its release, thanks to the shroud of mystery surrounding the universe in which it would be set. Since Nintendo's own communications had been almost disturbingly quiet on the subject, the run-up to its release on March 3, 2017, had seen a profusion of increasingly wild theories about its narrative setting and its place in the overall timeline of the saga. Fans began to see even the tiniest details as potentially vital evidence for this or that theory about the storyline of *Breath of the Wild*.

In hindsight, what's most interesting about the game is not so much the new secrets it reveals about the franchise as the way in which they're presented in the game. The specific narrative choices made in *Breath of the Wild* help it stand out from its predecessors by returning once again to its earliest origins. Focused entirely on providing players with an enjoyable experience, the story is mainly built around the gameplay and only serves up new narrative elements a drop or two at a time as our exploration draws us further and further out into the distant lands of Hyrule.

In this second chapter, we will lay out the narrative context that serves as the starting point for Link's adventure and then take a closer look at the various elements that make up the world of the game. Only after we have attempted to identify the game's key story elements through its leading protagonists and secondary characters will we turn to the finer details that could shed light on its potential connections to the overall timeline of the series. Our tour of *Breath of the Wild* then concludes with a section in which we consider why nature plays such a symbolic role in the world of the game, followed by an attempt to decode the musical atmosphere that permeates its different environments.

TRACES OF A PAINFUL PAST

BEFORE THE AWAKENING

In discussing their script for *Breath of the Wild*, Eiji Aonuma and his team often pointed out that giving the hero amnesia was the best way of putting players on an equal footing with the character they'd be playing. For example, just as Link has no memory of his past when he wakes up in the mysterious chamber where he was apparently placed without his knowledge, the player also has no idea of what their quest is all about. *What's my role? Why am I sleeping in this strange place in the middle of nowhere? When did they put me in this strange device? And what happened before that?* Players are faced with a dizzying flood of such questions from the very first moments of the game.

Although video game scriptwriters have long used amnesia as a one-size-fits-all plot device (Cloud in *Final Fantasy VII*, Kaim in *Lost Odyssey*, and Conrad in *Flashback* are among the most successful examples), it does offer certain obvious advantages. Playing as a hero who's already familiar with his or her situation often means that players have to sit through a cutscene or similar narrative introduction. Unfortunately, this also forces players to remain passive throughout the various explanations. Even if the character's background is only revealed to us a little at a time over the course of the story, every new element added to fill out the character's identity also tends to create an increasingly impersonal distance from the player. Because Link has amnesia, on the other hand, we learn who we are and what this world wants from us at the same time as he does, which immediately strengthens our identification with our hero. And even though, for the first time in the series, players can't choose their own name for their avatar, we've never felt more deeply engaged with the game. Because we have total freedom to approach the adventure however we like, the game immediately gives us a sense of being in control of our character, whose changing physical appearance reflects our progression through the game.

But let's get back to our story. As he climbs out of the mysterious box in which he seems to have been sleeping for an eternity, Link is guided by a woman's voice addressing him as the chosen one who is destined to save the world. Of course, that doesn't tell us anything about what might have happened in the past. Although the game is extremely stingy with narrative explanations throughout the adventure, we don't have to wait too long to learn the real story behind these events. By speaking with an old man who reveals his identity very early on, the player learns the true gravity of the situation at the same time as the hero and discovers its roots in a tragedy that took place over a century before. Another key character then appears to shed light on the cause of the disaster by recounting an ancient legend from ten thousand years ago. Since the present situation can only be explained as a consequence of the past century's events, which are in turn directly tied to the events of the distant past, having a global perspective on these three different periods helps find the answers to our questions.

Ten thousand years ago

According to an ancient legend, history has been repeating itself since time immemorial, closely intertwining the fate of Hyrule's royal family with that of Calamity Ganon, the incarnation of ultimate evil. Driven by an unquenchable thirst for power, this monster from the darkest depths of time returns in every cycle to threaten peace in the kingdom, forcing the princess and her appointed knight to rise up against and defeat him. For a long time, the alliance between these two sacred powers—one residing in the power of the purifying blade, and one a legacy passed down through Hyrule's royal family—was Link and Zelda's only option to seal this abomination away. Because they are imbued with the hero's soul and the blood of the goddess Hylia, these relics of past times have never failed to complete their quest, allowing history to repeat itself throughout the ages and keeping the kingdom safe. But each victory always came at the cost of a painful struggle, and so the events that took place ten thousand years ago were aimed at giving the army of Hyrule a decisive advantage. The kingdom's civilization was then at its peak, with no threats to its prosperity or its peaceful way of life. Taking advantage of this favorable situation, the people decided to get a head start on the next cycle by building powerful machines that would help the hero and the princess in the terrible confrontations to come. They created four Divine Beasts, formidable weapons of war controlled by elite pilots known as Champions. From that time forward, the kingdom had a considerable advantage against the Calamity, with the Divine Beasts as the ultimate weapons in a huge army that also included several hundred war machines called Guardians. These completely autonomous mechanical soldiers helped to protect the people of Hyrule and keep the demon in check. But with the passage of time, the legend came to be thought of as a mere folk tale and was ultimately forgotten as the ancient relics gradually disappeared underground, far from mortal eyes... That is, of course, unless they were intentionally buried out of sight in order to hide their existence from future generations, as suggested by a theory that we will discuss in greater detail in the next chapter.

The tragedy of the last century

In any case, the legend of the Divine Beasts was still passed down from generation to generation, and a century before the events of the game, the people were guided by a prophecy warning that the demon would soon return and revealing the existence of powerful machines that could be used to defeat him. Despite all that, the final battle against Ganon ended with a resounding victory for the demon! How could such a tragedy have happened when the people of Hyrule were supposed to have an enormous advantage over the enemy? In the end, that same overwhelming military force fell into the hands of the kingdom's adversaries, and the king's army was summarily routed. It seems that once the people of Hyrule had unearthed the relics of the past, they took their victory for granted and made the grave mistake of underestimating their enemy. They were then completely unprepared when the Calamity took down the four Champions who piloted the Divine Beasts, then seized control of both the Divine Beasts and the Guardians. Ganon found himself leading a swarm of deadly machines that were ready to turn against their own creators. After countless centuries of suffering defeat after defeat, the Calamity took his terrifying revenge, concentrating the destructive fire of his new mechanical soldiers on the defenders of the Sacred Realm, who were soundly defeated.

What became of the hero, the princess, and all those who stood beside them in those dark days? When Link awakens—and more precisely, at the moment when he learns of this tragedy through the stories told by two key characters who we'll return to a little later—almost no one has survived the century of suffering spent under Ganon's dominion. It is even stated quite clearly that the defeat of the Champions led to their deaths and that the same is also true of Link, who owes his survival entirely to the princess's decision to place him in the Shrine of Resurrection for one hundred long years, in hopes of future vengeance.

From that day on, Zelda has used what remains of her strength to stop Ganon's influence from spreading beyond the walls of Hyrule Castle, unsure of how long she would be able to contain him. And so, even though all he has is a handful of hazy memories and a keen sense of his own vulnerability in the devastated remains of Hyrule, our hero realizes that the destiny of the entire kingdom lies in his hands alone. To fulfill his role as the chosen one by ridding the world of the Calamity for good, he must first find a way to take back control of the ancient relics that are now in the enemy's hands and then help the princess to defeat the Calamity once and for all.

ALLIES AND PEOPLES OF HYRULE

LINK'S FIRST GUIDES

Although players are made to feel as though they're on their own for almost the entire game, *Breath of the Wild* still offers a small number of key characters to act as guides. Even in the absence of a real mentor, Link can still count on direct or indirect support from three individuals who provide him with important guidance during the earliest stages of his quest. Just as Zelda's voice roused the hero from his slumber at the start of *The Legend of Zelda: A Link to the Past* on the SNES, Link is again awakened by a distress call from the princess in *Breath of the Wild*. He again feels the same sense of urgency in her words—the sense that her only hope for saving her people is to rely completely on her appointed knight, even if her goal seems out of reach. The way that Zelda's character is handled in this episode and the role that she will play throughout the game, turn out to be so unique that we prefer to reserve our discussion of her for a separate section later on. For now, let us simply note that it is Zelda's mysterious call for help that allows Link to emerge from his long slumber and that the player connects with Link as soon as he opens his eyes to face the immensity of the quest that awaits him. Strictly speaking, there is nothing at that exact moment to actually prove that the voice guiding us is indeed Zelda's, but there's really no other possibility. As Link emerges from the Shrine of Resurrection, the same voice speaks to us as the "light of Hyrule," urging him to embark on his quest immediately, since he embodies the kingdom's only hope for recovering its former glory.

Any traveler could easily be gripped with panic at their first glimpse of the vast panorama that unfolds below the clifftop where Link first steps into the light. But a quick glance to the side reveals an unexpected visitor that we can't simply walk past without stopping to ask a few questions. Nearly the only part of him that is visible under his hooded garment is a prodigious white beard, evidence of a long and full life, and sparkling eyes that know much but say little. Describing himself as a slightly eccentric old man who has lived alone as a hermit for many years, he bears a certain resemblance to other quirky older fellows that we've encountered throughout the series. In the first *Zelda* game, Link often ran into strange old men in the most far-flung corners of the world, and they always had a bit of enigmatic advice to share. Any player who dared to go after these odd figures with a sword was quickly driven back by the magic torches that protected them. Omnipresent throughout the series, these wise old men have always symbolized the idea of knowledge that must be protected at any price.

The same is true of the hermit in *Breath of the Wild*, who refuses to reveal his precious knowledge until Link has completed a trial in which he must emerge victorious from four different shrines. This clever way of concealing the steps of what is actually little more than a tutorial, though presented in a much more intuitive way than usual, brings a sense of added breadth to the story—which doesn't truly start until this initial stage is complete. The old man can then share everything he knows with Link, from his own true identity to the nature of the challenge that awaits our hero, because he now has faith in Link's ability to save the kingdom. It turns out that this man is none other than the last King of Hyrule, Rhoam Bosphoramus—or rather, his ghost, the last vestige that remains of him after his armies were defeated by the Calamity. Perhaps the most telling symbol of the kingdom's collapse is the Temple of Time, which has stood in ruins for nearly a century. Completely abandoned after Ganon's victory over the people of Hyrule, this sacred place is much like every other part of the world: desolate and ruled by chaos. Virtually nothing remains of the kingdom, except for certain traces of the few who still attempt to survive within their respective tribes. As our hero listens to the former king, we learn that Link himself also perished one hundred years earlier, having fought until his last ounce of strength was gone. In the end, he only survived thanks to the efforts of the princess, who had ordered that he be placed in a special chamber in the Shrine of Resurrection. The voice that had guided him when he awoke was indeed that of Princess Zelda of Hyrule, since the former king's daughter is now the only one who can prevent Ganon from returning to his original form... but for how much longer?

This isn't the first time in the series that the king of Hyrule has hidden his identity from our hero by taking on a completely different appearance in order to act as his guide. For example, it's not until quite late in *The Wind Waker* that we learn the true nature of the King of Red Lions, the boat that is Link's main ally in this seafaring adventure. The mystical vessel turns out to be a reincarnation of the drowned former king, Daphnes Nohansen Hyrule. In *Breath of the Wild*, Link's meeting with Rhoam Bosphoramus Hyrule not only occurs much earlier, but is also quickly followed by revelations about the character. Everything happens as if to ensure that players are aware of the implications of their quest from very early on, so that they can then decide for themselves on the best way to complete it. Since the catastrophe has already occurred, there is no real sense of urgency, and although it's clear that the princess won't be able to contain Ganon's power for another century, no one urges Link to start his attack as soon as possible—in fact, the king advises him not to rush into things. To defeat the Calamity, Link must first take back control of the four Divine Beasts that the demon has seized for himself. Only then can he attempt to make his way into Hyrule Castle, which now serves as the monster's lair.

To learn more, Link will have to start by heading to Kakariko Village to meet a woman named Impa. She takes over from the late king to provide Link with the last few pieces of advice he'll need to fulfill his destiny. Over the course of the series, Impa is surely one of the characters who has gone through the most changes and developments. Originally described as Princess Zelda's kindly nursemaid, Impa becomes an increasingly important character from one episode to the next, and she plays a major role in *Ocarina of Time* as a young warrior. But when she's not out fighting evil as Zelda's bodyguard, the faithful Impa generally appears as an old woman in the series. Her role in that form is to share her knowledge with Link to help him save the princess. In *Skyward Sword*, Impa even appears in both forms at once: she disguises herself as the Elder, but her true identity is revealed by the long swinging braid that slips out from beneath her enormous hood.

Given that an entire century has passed, it makes sense that we meet a very elderly version of Impa when Link reaches Kakariko Village in *Breath of the Wild*. Talkative and surprisingly lively despite her withered body, the old woman still seems like she'd be able to handle herself in a fight and may remind some players of older characters in Rumiko Takahashi's manga work (like Shampoo's great-grandmother in *Ranma 1/2*)... but minus the sour-tempered attitude! The very embodiment of wisdom, Impa's main role is to help Link recover from his amnesia by embarking on a quest for the precious memories that connect him to the princess. This long side mission is entirely optional, but it is the only way to understand certain subtler aspects of the story that relate to Zelda's defeat one hundred years earlier. According to the elderly Impa, Link's life was hanging by a thread when Zelda made the decision to put him in an enchanted slumber. So there is a slight nuance distinguishing Impa's version of the story, in which Link was saved at the last moment, from the king's version, in which Link actually fought to the death before being brought back to life a century later. Be that as it may, Impa is one of the most iconic representatives of the Sheikah tribe in *Breath of the Wild*—and her tribe is more deeply involved in the storyline of this game than in any other episode in the series.

SHEIKAH TECHNOLOGY

According to King Rhoam Bosphoramus Hyrule, it took a full century for Link to come back to life after his remains were placed in a chamber in the Shrine of Resurrection. The success of this operation is nothing short of a miracle and provides an idea of the incredible potential of Sheikah technology. Much like *Horizon: Zero Dawn*, a game that combines primitive and futuristic elements in the same narrative universe, the world of *Breath of the Wild* is primarily a wild one in which nature has reasserted its authority, but traces of an advanced technology are still found everywhere we look.

First introduced in *Ocarina of Time*, the Sheikah are depicted as a "shadow tribe" with a similar role to that of the Japanese ninja caste known as *shinobi*. As the protectors of Hyrule's royal family, they possess formidable skills as warriors and closely resemble Hylians (the native inhabitants of the kingdom, of whom Link and Zelda are familiar examples) in their physical appearance.

They are distinguished by their red eyes, however, a unique feature that has become a symbol of their people, often represented in a drawing of a scarlet eye shedding a single tear of blood. *Breath of the Wild* is the first game in the series to present this tribe as a full-fledged community, finally providing us with a larger vision of who the Sheikah really are beyond the single character of Impa. Even more interestingly, we learn that within this same group, a certain number of individuals have betrayed the royal family to serve Ganon's cause. These hostile traitors wander the world under the banner of the Yiga Clan and are led by Master Kohga, a new character who will cross Link's path as part of his main quest. The idea of making this shadowy tribe into a secret society that includes rebels who might leap out to attack Link anywhere he goes adds a real sense of tension to his quest. Once players have been caught out the first time, they start to suspect that every NPC (non-player character) they meet could be trying to lure them into a trap—making exploration that much more exciting. But the Sheikah are primarily known for their ancestral knowledge and their seemingly magical artifacts, like the Lens of Truth that lets Link see otherwise invisible objects in *Ocarina of Time* and *Majora's Mask*. The setting of *Breath of the Wild* goes even further with the idea of presenting the Sheikah as the possessors of an advanced technology far beyond that of the other civilizations in this world. A few Sheikah scientists have survived the past century and are still alive in the present day, including Purah, Robbie and their assistants. Besides the Shrine of Resurrection that brought Link back to life after 100 years of restful sleep, the kingdom is home to no fewer than one hundred and twenty sacred places of the same type, carefully hidden in the game environment. They are all guarded by Sheikah monks who serve the goddess Hylia, and whose role is to present the chosen one with the Spirit Orbs reserved for those who successfully complete their trials.

Both inside and out, these futuristic-looking shrines clearly reflect the advanced state of Sheikah technology, which differs sharply from the otherwise primitive appearance of the world. This contrast may remind some players of the Olmec culture in the original *Mysterious Cities of Gold* animated series (a Franco-Japanese collaboration created by Jean Chalopin in 1982) and its technological contrast with the Inca and other pre-Columbian civilizations that Esteban, Tao and Zia encounter during their journey. Just as the local tribes and the Spaniards seemed to be thousands of years behind the Olmecs and the descendants of the Hiva (Mu) empire, the inhabitants of *Breath of the Wild* are also out of their depth when faced with Sheikah knowledge that only a select few can ever hope to understand. Forgotten for nearly ten thousand years, even the Sheikah tribe's most powerful inventions—the four Divine Beasts originally designed to serve the royal family—were ultimately turned against their creators.

One fan theory has it that this technology was not simply forgotten over time, but actively hidden from view. And indeed, on the map of Hyrule included with the US collector's edition of *Breath of the Wild* unveiled by Reggie Fils-Aimé, a hidden message refers to the Sheikah tribe's banishment by the reigning king of Hyrule at the time—a fearful reaction to the Divine Beasts' enormous firepower. These notes imply that the ancient weapons were intentionally buried so that future generations could never use them again. Terrified by the destructive power of these machines, the king even went so far as to persecute and banish the tribe that had designed them, leaving the Sheikah deeply resentful of the royal family. This might explain the appearance of the Yiga Clan, a band of traitors hostile to the kingdom of Hyrule, whose symbol is an upside-down Sheikah Eye.

Fortunately, not all of this exceptional people's creations wound up in enemy hands, and Link quickly acquires a unique tool that will allow him to reactivate this slumbering technology. That tool is the multipurpose Sheikah Slate, which—besides giving him access to various modules with surprising effects—is also the only way to activate the many shrines and gigantic towers buried in different locations around the world. Without the slate, Link would be unable to strengthen his abilities or overcome the obstacles in his path, let alone find his way through the vast environment, since activating the Sheikah towers is the only way to acquire a map of the world around him. This artifact is also our hero's only chance to prove his identity to those who are not ready to believe that the chosen one has returned.

Sadly, just like every other advanced civilization, the Sheikah could not resist the urge to use their unparalleled knowledge to develop powerful war machines. This led to the creation of the Guardians—a swarm of autonomous mechanical soldiers that could do battle with no need for human intervention, manufactured by the hundred in distinct (but equally fearsome) ground- and air-based variants. Although their design differs considerably from one type to the next, the Guardians owe their general appearance to that of the Octoroks; these monsters have been a part of the series since the beginning and inspired the designers with their imposing size relative to Link as they appeared in the first game. The overall Sheikah style was inspired by the Jōmon era, a very ancient and little-known period of Japanese history (dating from about 15,000 to 3,000 BCE) during which the first Japanese pottery appeared. In a "making of" video released shortly after the game came out, artistic director Satoru Takizawa explains that the Sheikah Slate, the shrines, and all the ancient items and structures in the game reflect the aesthetic of the Jōmon period. This period was chosen to define the antique Sheikah civilization because of its unique character and the sense of mystery and wonder it brings with it, even for Japanese audiences. Cherry, the robot built by Robbie the scientist at the

Akkala Ancient Tech Lab, also bears a striking resemblance to the Jōmon-era figures exhibited at the Tokyo National Museum.

The ultimate achievement of Sheikah technology was the creation of the Divine Beasts, gigantic war machines designed to resemble huge animals. They were intended to save the kingdom, but ultimately led to its downfall ten thousand years later.

The Champions, masters of the Divine Beasts

By following in their ancestors' footsteps in their attempt to fulfill the ten-thousand-year-old prophecy, the king and his people accidentally armed the demon with the very weapon that was intended to destroy him. But no one could have expected such a disaster when all the conditions seemed right for the relics to return and protect the kingdom of Hyrule. After all, a similar strategy had worked ten thousand years earlier. Unlike the Guardian armies, designed by the Sheikah to act independently, the Divine Beasts were controlled by four "pilots" known as the Champions. Selected for their talent, these four individuals from four different tribes (Zoras, Gorons, Ritos, and Gerudos) were placed under the combined command of the princess and a fifth Champion, the appointed knight of the kingdom. In fact, Link's role was even more important in that he served as the leader of the four representatives of the peoples of Hyrule, with all five Champions under Zelda's authority. Each of the Divine Beasts possessed unimaginable firepower and controls designed to take full advantage of their animal designs (elephant, salamander, eagle, and camel), so their victory seemed all but assured.

And yet, ten thousand years later, during the reign of King Rhoam Bosphoramus, the four Champions were unable to overcome the enemy—and so they perished. Mipha piloted the Divine Beast known as Vah Ruta. This somewhat introspective Zora princess, daughter of King Dorephan and sister of Prince Sidon, was gifted with the ability to heal others. As a sign of her love for Link, whom she had known one hundred years before his awakening at the start of the game, she made him a tunic that allowed him to swim up waterfalls. Daruk, of the Goron tribe, controlled Vah Rudania. Representing the values of this warrior people with their home in the mountains, he was respected for his bravery and prodigious strength. After his death, he was held up as an ideal role model for his people. Revali, of the Ritos tribe, was the pilot for Vah Medoh. Unlike the other Champions, his proud and provocative character might have roused feelings of distrust in Link, but his brazen self-confidence was merely a front for a healthy sense of rivalry. Finally, Urbosa, the Gerudo Champion, was in charge of Vah Naboris. Her athletic warrior's build and protective nature, similar to the traits that defined Impa's character in *Ocarina of Time*, were supplemented by her unique ability to summon lightning around her. Despite their abilities, the four warriors failed to push back the phantoms of Ganon, which defeated them and took control of their Divine Beasts a century before the events of the game.

It is interesting to note that the names of the four Divine Beasts come from key characters well known to fans of the series, and that each one represents a particular tribe: Ruto (the Zora princess) for Vah Ruta, Darunia (chief of the Gorons) for Vah Rudania, Nabooru (a Gerudo sage) for Vah Naboris, and Medli (a member of the Ritos tribe) for Vah Medoh. The first three characters are from *Ocarina of Time*, while Medli is from *The Wind Waker*.

Not only did the four Divine Beasts fail to protect the Kingdom, they were also corrupted by Ganon, who then had complete control of them. This is why Link has to seek the support of Hyrule's major tribes in order to approach these gigantic mechanical creatures in hopes of making his way inside them and taking control from within.

THE PEOPLE OF HYRULE

Ever since *Ocarina of Time*, Hyrule's population has become increasingly diverse, and the series has introduced a growing number of NPCs from the various tribes. Of course, each title has its own more or less distinct vision of these different peoples, but we can still identify certain elements that have remained constant in most games after the Nintendo 64 episode. Therefore, players won't be surprised to see that the Zoras, Gorons and Gerudos in *Breath of the Wild* are generally quite similar to their counterparts in *Ocarina of Time*. As for the Ritos people, they were first introduced in *The Wind Waker*, and their presence in the world of *Breath of the Wild* is one of the biggest surprises in this episode, as we will see in greater detail in a later section about the game's place in the overall timeline of the series. In any case, the story of *Breath of the Wild* revolves around these four main tribes, once Link sets out on his quest to find the people who once knew the former Champions and who should be able to lead him to the Divine Beasts and subsequently bring them under his control.

The intentionally free-form structure of this episode's open world means that players can complete this main quest in any way they like. In other words, it's entirely possible to seek out any of the four tribes right from the very beginning of the game and to approach the Divine Beasts in whatever order we choose. For that matter, we might also choose not to free any of them at all! The order in which we have chosen to discuss the different tribes here is therefore purely arbitrary.

Appearing for the first time as NPCs and enemies in *A Link to the Past*, then cropping up regularly in later episodes (*Ocarina of Time, Majora's Mask, The Wind Waker, Twilight Princess, A Link Between Worlds*), the Zoras are a race of hybrid creatures who live in aquatic environments. It is generally accepted that the Zoras who are initially presented as monsters in early episodes of the series are distinct from the resolutely peaceful people we get to know later on. Recognizable by their webbed feet, large fins and fish-tailed heads, the Zoras acquire an even more diverse range of character designs in *Breath of the Wild*, and some of the individuals we meet in the game have a truly unique appearance. Zora society is organized as a traditional monarchy, with its members swearing allegiance to a king who is generally much physically larger than his subjects. King Dorephan leads the Zoras at the time of the events of the game, and he sends his son, Prince Sidon, to ask for Link's help after his daughter Mipha had lost her life in the battle that took place a century before. Although the royal family doesn't blame him for his failure, the same cannot be said for all Zoras, some of whom still harbor a fierce hatred for the "chosen one" who was supposed to protect their princess. Due to the Zoras' exceptional longevity, most of the people who were there to witness the tragedy of the past century are still alive in the present day. It is therefore no surprise that the people who knew Mipha personally now feel bitter resentment toward Link, whom they also remember from those dark days. In their eyes, the hero failed to complete his appointed task and is therefore responsible for the death of their princess. Fortunately, Prince Sidon quickly becomes a reliable and encouraging ally for Link in his attempt to approach Vah Ruta, the Divine Beast that Mipha had tried to defend at the cost of her own life.

North of Zora's Domain, not far from Death Mountain, another tribe has made its home inside the mines, undisturbed by the lava's heat. They are, of course, none other than the Gorons, well known to fans of the franchise since *Ocarina of Time* thanks to their frequent appearances in subsequent episodes. Here again, the way in which the tribe is presented in *Breath of the Wild* holds few surprises, with the Gorons we meet in this game closely resembling the ones we've encountered elsewhere in the series. While reaching Goron City is no easy matter due to the intense heat that permeates the volcanic landscape around it, Link needs to get there in order to save the person who will lead him to the Divine Beast Vah Rudania. Harassed by a gang of hulking Moblins, a timid Goron named Yunobo is waiting to be rescued by our hero so that he can follow in the footsteps of his valiant ancestor Daruk, the Champion who died a century earlier. This is the first time in the series that we meet a Goron character who is presented as fragile and fearful, since this tribe is generally known for its incredible strength, with bodies as solid as stone. The journey to find Vah Rudania is therefore an especially challenging one for this offbeat pair.

Far away to the southwest, at the opposite corner of the world, the Gerudo tribe resides in a town exposed to the suffocating heat of the desert. Since men (known as *voe* in the local tongue) are not allowed inside, this city is not especially welcoming for Link, who is forced to disguise himself as a woman in order to meet with their young chief, Riju. As a descendant of Urbosa, the Gerudo Champion from the previous century, Riju agrees to help Link, but not before demanding a favor from the chosen one who claims to have known her ancestor. Only after Link has recovered the Thunder Helm from the Yiga clan will the young queen give him what he needs to approach the Divine Beast known as Vah Naboris. Because of its direct link to the origins of Ganondorf (Ganon's humanoid form), well-established since *Ocarina of Time*, the Gerudo tribe of warrior women plays a very interesting role in the series. Legend has it that only one Gerudo male is born each century and that he is inevitably destined to become their king, as was the case with Ganondorf. This point is not directly addressed in *Breath of the Wild*, but we do encounter a number of Gerudo women who are preparing to leave their hometown to find potential husbands from another race, usually Hylians.

Inseparably associated with the world of *The Wind Waker*, where they were presented as descendants of the Zora people (according to the official history in *Hyrule Historia* published by Dark Horse Books), the Ritos tribe makes an unexpected return in *Breath of the Wild*. Because the Zoras are also present in this episode, simply finding the two races coexisting side-by-side raises certain questions about where *Breath of the Wild* fits into the overall timeline of the series—but we'll return to this issue later on. Physically, the Ritos people resemble birds with humanoid characteristics. In fact, the name *Ritos* is an anagram of *tori*, the Japanese word for birds. In *Breath of the Wild*, Link must make his way through the high mountains surrounding Ritos Village in order to meet with Kaneli, the village elder. There, he is presented with another trial and must prove his skill as an archer before attempting to approach the Divine Beast Vah Medoh, which killed its Champion, Revali.

Although they are only a secondary tribe in *Breath of the Wild*, living far away from the prying eyes of strangers, the Korok tribe is another element inherited directly from *The Wind Waker*. Intended to represent an evolution of the Kokiri children introduced in *Ocarina of Time*, the Koroks are strange half-plant, half-humanoid creatures, their faces hidden behind large leaf masks, who reside in a sacred forest. These children of nature are only optionally involved in the story of *Breath of the Wild*, depending on whether or not the player decides to seek the legendary sword. In addition, there are no fewer than nine hundred individual Koroks hidden throughout the world, hiding in all manner of strange places to avoid being spotted by the other inhabitants of Hyrule. Although they don't expect anyone to find them, they never complain about giving up one of their precious seeds to whoever manages to flush them out.

Despite its immense size, the world of *Breath of the Wild* feels incredibly alive due to the many types of people and animals who live in it. The diversity of the tribes we encounter and especially the fact that every individual we meet is already going about their daily business before Link comes along, helps to make the world feel much more believable as a place where life goes on independently of our actions. Most NPCs in *Breath of the Wild* travel from place to place at different times of the day, and some of them have no problem leaving their villages behind to travel many miles on foot or on horseback into the hostile countryside. The idea of giving NPCs a specific daily schedule arose when the team realized that certain characters were showing illogical behavior that could break immersion for players, like walking around late at night despite the risk of being devoured by the undead skeletons that have a bothersome habit of bursting forth from the ground. This tidbit comes from an interview with Eiji Aonuma and Shigeru Miyamoto in which the two creators explained that they focused on details like these out of a concern for realism. As for the stables where Link can register his horses, they were imagined as trading posts for various characters in the game—meeting places where people from different races and far-flung villages come to interact. Link also runs into a certain wandering merchant named Beedle at these stables, having met him for the first time in *The Wind Waker*. Fortunately, players don't need to know the ins and outs of every episode in the series to appreciate *Breath of the Wild*, but it is nevertheless filled with interesting references to earlier *Zelda* games, starting with the map of the world that consists almost entirely of names that recall places or characters from other installments in the series.

ZELDA'S CHARACTER

While she plays an unusual role in *Breath of the Wild*, intervening only indirectly in present-day events, Princess Zelda drives the narrative of this episode almost entirely by herself. She is no longer the harmless young lady patiently awaiting her savior that we met in the first *Zelda* game; nor is she the mysterious heroine who disguised her true identity behind the character of

Sheik in *Ocarina of Time* or in a very different way in *The Wind Waker* as the energetic young pirate named Tetra. And she seems even less like the heroic and valiant figure who boldly took up her sword to defend her kingdom in *Twilight Princess*. In *Breath of the Wild*, the treatment of Princess Zelda upends everyone's expectations by completely redefining the young woman's character, humanizing her more effectively than in any other episode in the saga.

The scriptwriters' surprising decision to present the game's story as if it were little more than a long shadow cast by the events of the previous century—and more specifically, the direct consequence of a much more serious crisis—makes the player eager to learn more about what happened in those days. While we learn early on that the chaos we see in today's world results from the failure of the armies of Hyrule to stop the Calamity a hundred years before, the details of their defeat are intentionally hidden from us, though it is implied that they were much more dramatic than the events of the present day. These revelations are doled out in bits and pieces in a small number of flashbacks, presented as memories that we have to find for ourselves by hunting for Hyrule's most carefully-hidden secrets around the margins of the main story. In fact, there is nothing to prevent us from moving along to the game's narrative conclusion fairly quickly, although this would also mean leaving most of these secrets still buried in unexplored regions of the world. For the first time, then, a *Zelda* episode invites us to accept the idea that the most interesting part of the game lies off the beaten path of its main storyline, in the distant reaches of a world that we come to master even as the hero clears away the thick fog that clouds his memory. Link's amnesia certainly won't stop him from accomplishing his goal, but who would really want to finish the game without unraveling the mystery of the century-old tragedy in which Zelda apparently failed to complete the sacred mission that had been entrusted to her?

So it's mainly through these fragmented memories, presented as brief flashbacks scattered throughout the world and appearing in no particular order, that we discover the key moments that led the battle of the previous century to the disastrous ending we already know. Just as players can explore the game's various dungeons in any order they choose, we only stumble onto one of these precious memories at random or sometimes after a grueling search. The only clues we have to help us find them are a dozen photographs, each showing the precise location where a particular scene took place. And while it might seem at first that these visual indications would be sufficiently clear to let us readily guess where each memory is located, the staggering immensity of the world—and more importantly, the ways in which that world has changed over the past 100 years—make the task far more difficult than it appears. A statue seen in one of the photos might well have been demolished after Ganon took control of the Guardians, or a bridge in another might have been partially destroyed.

Besides turning the search for memories into a genuine treasure hunt that will keep Link busy for days on end, another advantage of superimposing parallel visions of the past and the present is that it makes us more conscious of the visual impact of the tragedy. The environment itself has been badly scarred by the chaos that has unfurled over the land of Hyrule and stripped of much of its former majesty and beauty. As a result, we find ourselves following the traces of Hyrule's past glory as if on a pilgrimage in memory of those who were unjustly lost, accompanied by an unceasing desire to find out what happened to Princess Zelda herself.

As the starting point for all of these lost memories, the game's take on the relationship between the future queen of the kingdom and her appointed knight wipes the slate clean, abandoning all the clichés that had previously connected the two. In viewing these scenes from the past, we quickly sense a sharp conflict between Link and Zelda—a discovery made all the more troubling and confusing by the fact that we acquire these memories out of order. The more we see of these flashbacks, the more we wonder what could have caused such uncharacteristic tensions between these two great figures of the past, with the princess displaying an unrelentingly icy attitude toward the hero whom we struggle to imagine ever doing her wrong. This conflict raises the possibility of a story in which the purity and perfection of the Zelda character are chipped away to reveal a more believable and human personality. After all, despite her role as a future queen, Zelda is still a young woman like any other—a young woman tormented by the fear of failing to complete the task she has been asked to bear, questioning her own abilities in a thousand different ways, and eventually turning the anger she feels toward herself upon her loyal appointed knight. From one memory to the next, we see Zelda crushed under the weight of her responsibilities, suffering and even crying as she feels the completion of her quest slipping away from her. The distraught young woman cannot even count on the support of her own father, since Rhoam Bosphoramus is primarily concerned with the health of his kingdom and displays an almost cruel lack of sensitivity to his daughter's plight, refusing to accept the possibility that she might fail. In the same way, Zelda sees Link as a devoted protector, but one who is incapable of truly understanding her; she nearly goes so far as to put the weight of her own mistakes on him, since she can't stand the thought of being the only one responsible for the impending tragedy.

Zelda's character in *Breath of the Wild* is surprising because she seems more human than ever, with human faults and weaknesses, as opposed to the infallible character presented in earlier games—a combination of purity, dignity, courage, and vitality who was generally the key to the final battle against Ganon. Seeing

Princess Zelda overcome by emotions like anger or jealousy, simply because she doesn't feel worthy of the task entrusted to her when everyone else around her seems infallible, is a first for the series. Sensitive and vulnerable, the Zelda we meet in *Breath of the Wild* evokes a more emotional response than any other character in the story, and her inner torment has a much greater impact on the player than the feats of all the previous Zelda characters combined.

MEMORIES TO UNTANGLE THE THREADS OF THE PAST

Intended as an event of great importance for the kingdom, the ceremony in which Princess Zelda officially dubs Link as her appointed knight by giving him the goddess Hylia's blessing instead rings false—so much so that the four Champions in attendance find the whole spectacle to be strangely grim. The young woman pronounces the words of the ritual in a trembling and uncertain voice, as if reciting a tired litany that she doesn't really believe in. Revali, the Ritos Champion, even goes so far as to point out Zelda's lack of interest in the young knight, whose presence she does not especially seem to appreciate. But the Gerudo Champion, Urbosa, counters that the most likely reason for Zelda's coolness toward Link is that everything about him reminds her of her own shortcomings. With his skill in combat and unbreakable will, Link is clearly destined to become the hero of Hyrule, the chosen one with the purifying blade who will slay Ganon, the Calamity. But Zelda will also have her own role to play when the moment comes, and she seems to have grave doubts about her ability to complete her appointed task. In a memory focused on Daruk, Champion of the Gorons, we learn that the decision to place Link in the role of Zelda's personal knight was made by the king himself, with no regard for his daughter's wishes, which clearly doesn't make things any easier between the two young people. Urbosa says that every time Zelda sets eyes on Link's sword, her heart fills with dread over her own weakness and the thought of dishonoring her family.

From her earliest childhood, Zelda has spared no effort in pursuing her duty, spending long hours meditating in icy spring waters with no thought of her own health, in hopes of one day seeing her true power emerge. But those efforts were in vain. Even so, rather than simply lamenting her fate, the princess decides very early on to dedicate her time to what she is best at, spending entire days studying ancient relics until her eyes droop with exhaustion. Amid the kingdom's ancient columns, Zelda realizes that the ruins of the Sheikah shrines will only open to the chosen one with the purifying blade and that she herself cannot enter. Link arrives just at that moment, and Zelda's feeling of injustice leads her to reject him, telling him she has no need of his services—even though her protector has come to her by order of the king. But Zelda's proud and haughty manner is only an act; in reality, she is simply furious at being unable to lead her life the way she wants to. While we sympathize with Link over her severe treatment of him when he is only doing his duty, we also sense that behind her anger, the princess is struggling to hide her own suffering.

In fact, Zelda's knowledge of Sheikah technology far surpasses that of anyone else in the kingdom. She has a perfect understanding of how the ancient weapons work and can modify Divine Beasts to make them even more effective, but she wants to go further and discover all their secrets. This is her way of preparing for the confrontation with Ganon by convincing herself that she's on the right track. But her father, King Rhoam Bosphoramus, sees her efforts as little more than a self-indulgent whim and feels that she's wasting her time and energy on a task better left to others. He would rather see his daughter concentrating exclusively on the manifestation of her power.

Throughout all of these flashback sequences, Zelda has the Sheikah Slate in her hands, fascinated by the technology that (among other things) allows her to collect images of all of Hyrule's plant life. For example, we see her taking a picture of a symbolic flower known as the "silent princess." Sensing the tragic fate that awaits her, Zelda compares herself to this lovely flower, which seems doomed to extinction despite valiant efforts to preserve it. This explains why the same flower appears in such a symbolic way in the logo for Western versions of the game and on the pedestal that holds the legendary sword in the European collector's edition. This is also one of the rare moments in which we see Zelda having fun in Link's presence, as she extols the culinary virtues of a toad that she tries to make him eat while teasingly suggesting that his exceptional physical fitness makes him a perfect candidate for the experiment... The connection between our hero and the princess he is sworn to protect also grows stronger as the two ride along side-by-side. It seems that Link has taught Zelda to be gentler and more patient with her steed after a rocky start. The princess also remembers how her protector saved her from an ambush by the Yiga clan, appearing out of nowhere when she was about to perish on the assassins' blades. Gradually, the jealousy and rejection that she felt toward the knight forced upon her by her father give way to healthier emotions. In her moments of uncertainty, the princess even wonders what Link would have done in her place and what path he would have followed if he had not been blessed with the talents needed to complete his task.

At the Spring of Power, we learn that the sealing power which has been passed down from mother to daughter for generations in the royal family of Hyrule is the only way to stop the Calamity. This sacred power can only be awakened through prayer, requiring Zelda to pray at the feet of many different statues of the goddess Hylia. But the young woman feels nothing of the mystical power that is supposed to reside within her, nor does she hear the voices of the spirits that her grandmother once told her about. All she feels is a terrible sense of doubt that she will be able to fulfill her role when the moment comes. Although she is beginning to lose hope of ever finding a way to awaken this elusive power, she goes to the Spring of Wisdom on Mount Lanayru in the hope that her wish might be fulfilled. After all, according to the mythology of the series, Zelda has always been the keeper of the Triforce of Wisdom, while Link holds the Triforce of Courage and Ganon the Triforce of Power. So it would make sense for *Breath of the Wild* to draw on the lore of earlier games by designating the princess of Hyrule as the heir to the power of Nayru, goddess of Wisdom. But once again, nothing happens.

Zelda's anguish over her own powerlessness is revealed with striking poignancy as she and Link flee desperately through the woods after the armies of Hyrule fail in their efforts to stop the Calamity. Covered in mud and soaked to the skin in her fine white dress, the princess cannot hold back her tears as she realizes that all is lost. Link tries in vain to comfort her, but it's too late; the Divine Beasts and the Guardians have turned against them, and now Ganon has the upper hand. Zelda takes full responsibility for Hyrule's failure, blaming herself for being unable to harness the sealing power in time to stop the enemy. Everyone she loved has died because of her, including the Champions, trapped inside their own Divine Beasts.

Zelda's difficulty in awakening her powers might be explained by the fact that she lost her mother when she was just six years old, as her father mentions in an old book of his memories found in the ruins of Hyrule Castle. With no guide to show her the way, she was left to her own devices as she worked to realize her potential—but the only result was ten years of failure. Despite criticism from members of the court who saw her as a failed and irresponsible princess, Zelda managed to keep going by turning her attention to research, a reflection of her great strength of spirit. These memories also help to soften our view of the king's insensitive and demanding attitude toward his daughter during this period, as he admits his regrets over having forced her to endure ten years of strict discipline for the good of the kingdom. He even says that he won't hold it against her if she fails and that he will return to his role as a father to comfort her.

It is not until the thirteenth hidden memory, accessible only after discovering the twelve optional flashbacks at the locations shown on the photographs, that we finally see Zelda's powers awaken. During her desperate flight through the woods with her protector, she courageously steps between Link and the Guardian that has our young hero in its sights, refusing to let him die after she has finally learned to appreciate his worth. At that precise moment, her sealing power manifests itself, surrounding Zelda in a golden light that allows her to drive away the corruption of the ancient weapons thanks to the Triforce of Wisdom which appears on the back of her hand. The Guardians collapse lifelessly to the ground, and Link finds himself at the brink of death as the princess collects herself. It's here that Zelda's role turns out to be especially crucial, as she takes the initiative to place Link in suspended animation so that he can be resurrected in the future. And it's Zelda who decides to hide the legendary sword in the Korok Forest, under the protection of the Great Deku Tree. Encouraged by the glow of the purifying blade, the royal priestess of Hyrule shows by her actions that all is not yet lost in her eyes. More importantly, she still has faith in her appointed knight, even though he has forgotten every detail of his past by the time he reawakens a century later.

ZELDA'S JOURNAL AND LINK'S SILENCE

As if any proof were needed that the creators of *Breath of the Wild* were eager to disguise the details of what had happened in the past, a number of important revelations about certain protagonists appear only in old journal pages that are all too easy to miss. For example, this is how we learn the backstory of the Sheikah scientists who survived the catastrophe of the last century and escaped to laboratories at the outer fringes of the kingdom. But what we're most interested in here are the private thoughts that Princess Zelda wrote in her journal at the time, revealing her concerns about Link's characteristically silent manner. As we have seen, the relationship between the princess and her appointed knight gradually transforms as the young woman learns not to direct her own inner anger at the man who is, after all, only there to protect her. But as we read through the pages of her private journal, we realize that Zelda's frustration with our hero is also partly due to the weighty silences that dominate their every conversation.

From an external point of view, of course, Link's silence is simply a result of the saga's insistence on never allowing its main character to speak, in order to strengthen the player's identification with the hero. So although we're perfectly aware that Link is neither mute nor autistic, his interactions with NPCs are always wordless, and those he speaks with invariably manage to guess the hero's response even though he never actually says it out loud. In *Breath of the Wild*, however, the situation is a bit more complicated. For the first time in the series, the main characters are voiced by real actors in the most important narrative sequences. As a result, the fact that Link never responds directly to the princess when the two are interacting may seem vaguely disturbing. Even so, the designers could have easily just glossed this over, since players are generally able to select dialogue options, which clearly imply that Link is, in fact, able to speak, even if he's not especially talkative. But the team seems to have decided that it would be fun to push this issue a little farther by using Link's silence to further highlight Zelda's exasperation with a knight who is apparently unwilling to communicate with her.

The princess's journal is therefore filled with amusing examples of the strong tension that she feels whenever Link is around. After returning from her visit to Goron City, she writes (without ever using Link's name), "I still recall feeling his eyes on me as I walked ahead, and I grew anxious and weary. It is the same feeling I've felt before in his company... And still, not a word passes his lips. I never know what he's thinking! Then, I suppose it's simple. What does the boy chosen by the sword that seals the darkness think of me? A daughter of Hyrule's royal family yet unable to use sealing magic... He must despise me." Later, we read, "I said something awful to him today... My research was going nowhere. I was feeling depressed, and I had told him repeatedly not to accompany me. But he did anyway, as he always does, and so I yelled at him without restraint. He seemed confused by my anger. I feel terribly guilty... and that guilt only makes me more agitated then I was before." And finally, her agitation gradually evolves into a form of respect and admiration: "I am unsure how to put today's events into words. Words so often evade me lately, and now more than ever. He saved me. He protected me from the ruthless blades of the Yiga Clan. Though I've been cold to him all this time... taking my selfish and childish anger out on him at every turn... Still, he was there for me. I won't ever forget that. Tomorrow, I shall apologize for all that has transpired between us. And then... I will try talking to him. To Link. It's worth a shot." From then on, the two young people start opening up to one another and sharing special moments that we unfortunately never get to see in the game. Then she asks the all-important question: "When I finally got around to asking why he's so quiet all the time, I could tell it was difficult for him to say. But he did. With so much at stake and so many eyes upon him, he feels it necessary to stay strong and to silently bear any burden. I always believed him to be simply a gifted person who had never faced a day of hardship. How wrong I was... Everyone has struggles that go unseen by the world... I was so absorbed with my own problems, I failed to see his." Thus we learn that the lack of communication between the two protagonists had led to a terrible misunderstanding, which could have torn Zelda and Link apart forever if they hadn't found ways to gradually defuse it.

Ultimately, the most amusing part of all this—besides the decision to provide a specific explanation for Link's reluctance to speak—is how unfounded Zelda's concerns about him are. How could Link ever feel the least bit of contempt for the woman that he lives to protect, even above and beyond his official mission? In any case, seeing the princess torture herself with these thoughts shows how important it is to her to prove herself worthy of her appointed knight's devotion and to avoid disappointing him. This unexpected and poignant link between the saga's two leading figures is one of the most pleasant surprises in *Breath of the Wild*.

THEORIES ABOUT THE TIMELINE

A CONTROVERSIAL TIMELINE

Probably because most other grand sagas use a narrative model built around a strict overall timeline, the *Zelda* franchise eventually came around to adopting the same approach. But until the official encyclopedia *Hyrule Historia* was published in 2013, the series was known for setting off fiery but apparently futile debates around different potential chronologies. After all, hadn't the *Zelda* saga always gone out of its way to start over from scratch with each new episode, wiping out earlier narrative decisions to write a new story each time about the sacred battle for possession of the Triforce? Most fans therefore believe that each new episode features an entirely new Link, not a single hero with various past experiences based on his earlier adventures.

While it's difficult to come up with a clear answer to this question, especially considering that there clearly are real narrative connections between certain episodes, it's hard to avoid the conclusion that a single overall timeline for the entire *Zelda* saga was not part of Nintendo's original plan. But faced with the many theories proposed by fans to position this or that game relative to others in the series—some of which were truly off-the-wall—and probably also out of a concern for bringing a greater sense of cohesion to the franchise, Nintendo eventually revealed its own chronology so that everyone would finally be on the same page. Was this timeline already in place from the very beginning of the saga, evolving over time to provide a starting point for the writers of each new game? Or was it quickly slapped together in 2013 to put a lid on the most preposterous fan theories? We may never know for sure. The fact remains that by presenting a clear and detailed official timeline in the respectable encyclopedia entitled *Hyrule Historia*, with none other than Eiji Aonuma himself as the editorial director, Nintendo had provided its fans with a sacred tome of reference.

Published after the release of *Skyward Sword*, the encyclopedia explains that that episode marks the beginning of a legend, which, rather than proceeding in a strictly linear fashion over time, quickly splits off into three separate branches. The explanation for this is that the official timeline makes a major temporal distinction starting at the end of *Ocarina of Time*, resulting in three parallel timelines. Therefore, each of the episodes that come chronologically after *Ocarina of Time* falls into one of these three timelines, depending on two factors: the outcome of the battle between Link and Ganon and (if the Hero of Time wins that battle) whether it falls in the child or adult timeline.

Besides the relative complexity of this three-way timeline, which makes it a delicate matter for fans to decide on their own where any given episode should be placed in the overall branching structure of the series, we might also ask whether it was even necessary to establish an official chronology in the first place. Where players were once divided over how to arrange the various episodes with respect to one another, the debate was now whether the official timeline should actually be taken seriously. Does it reflect a cohesive narrative structure that goes back to the beginning of the saga, or is it simply the awkward result of an ill-advised move by Nintendo? Those who take the latter point of view argue that the division into three branches is too clumsy and point out that Nintendo didn't seem to care about an official timeline at all for many years, casting its overall relevance into serious doubt. In fact, the encyclopedia itself notes that "the interpretation of Hyrule's history is in constant evolution" and that "contradictions may arise as to the origins of certain events." Looking forward, "there is no doubt that this chronology is likely to see other changes in years to come," because "future legends may add new branches and change events that had previously been considered as well-established facts."

Clearly, then, this chronology should be taken with a grain of salt, in part because certain elements in *Breath of the Wild* reveal contradictions that are problematic for the official timeline, as we will see later. Whether or not we choose to believe in this official timeline, it deserves to be included at least briefly in our discussion of *Breath of the Wild*, even though the game's place in the overall timeline is ultimately of little importance.

The role of narrative in the *Zelda* franchise

While the major recurring themes that define the *Zelda* saga are probably already fairly clear, we can't really start our discussion of the storyline before relating the events of the third installment, *A Link to the Past*. The first two episodes for the NES came out at a time when story was still only an afterthought in video games and did little more than set up a basic fantasy environment featuring three main characters. Link, an elf-like hero instantly recognizable by his green tunic and pointy ears, had to defeat the guardians of eight different dungeons to collect all the pieces of the Triforce, a relic in the shape of a golden triangle, which he would then use to stop the evil Ganon's scheme and rescue Zelda, the princess of the kingdom. And in fact, unless players carefully pored over the story details laid out in the manuals for the first two games, there were very few in-game dialogues or cutscenes that went much beyond that initial statement of the premise.

With *A Link to the Past*, the outlines of the saga's mythology started to come into slightly sharper focus. The stakes are higher, and the very nature of the mysterious golden triangle—which, as we learn in this episode, is tied to the powers of three goddesses symbolizing power, wisdom and courage—starts to add a bit more narrative weight to the *Zelda* universe. In the hands of people with pure and noble intentions, the Triforce can provide a peaceful future for the kingdom of Hyrule. But if an evil creature gains control of it, darkness will descend upon the world. By touching the golden triangle even though his heart did not hold an equal balance of the three symbolic values demanded by the original goddesses, Ganon opened the gates to a world of darkness and shattered the power of the Triforce into three parts, keeping only the Triforce of Power for himself. This is why our villain is actively searching for the two other chosen ones, those who bear the symbols of wisdom (Zelda) and courage (Link), in hopes of restoring the omnipotent power of the golden triangle.

With *Ocarina of Time*, the legend became richer still, introducing more characters and revealing the existence of different tribes who would help to make this world much livelier and less predictable as the saga continued to unfold. Even so, the series is not especially well-known for the richness of its story—although it never really sought to compete with the complexity and tragedy of the stories told in RPGs, for example. For Nintendo, the narrative always takes a back seat to questions of player enjoyment; the story must serve the gameplay and adapt to its constraints. Most studios specializing in the development of role-playing or adventure games take precisely the opposite approach in this regard.

Throughout the series, then, the emphasis has clearly been more on entertaining the player than on any desire to surprise and shock them with unexpected revelations. Of course, the recurring question of Princess Zelda's hidden identity provides one of the main dramatic twists in certain episodes (*Ocarina of Time*, *The Wind Waker*), but big story beats like these are generally much less common than opportunities to impress the player with purely visual surprises. This approach is also reflected in the general tendency for each NPC we meet to have a crazier character design than the one before, to the point where it almost becomes disturbing. Over time, the lands of Hyrule became home to various unsettling creatures (Tingle, the strange character obsessed with forest fairies, the Great Fairies from the Nintendo 64 episodes, and Ooccoo and the Ooccas from *Twilight Princess*, who look like something straight out of Tod Browning's movie *Freaks*), as if Nintendo took some kind of twisted pleasure in making players experience the same sense of shock as Link when faced with various uncomfortable situations.

In short, what makes the world of *Zelda* such a fascinating setting is not so much its narrative aspects as the main characters and second-tier NPCs who bring it to life. But *Breath of the Wild* takes a different and unexpected approach to the story, which is presented in very different ways for the two distinct eras in which its events take place. While the story set in the present unfolds by way of the usual encounters with the inhabitants of Hyrule, the parts set in the past are revealed only in memories that Link discovers in various far-flung regions of the world. As we have already mentioned, this choice represents an entirely new direction for the series, and while some fans have questioned its appropriateness, there's no denying that it offers a perfectly viable response to the problems of telling a story in a game that players can explore in any order they like.

On this point, Eiji Aonuma has explained that he was worried that telling the story in too rigid a way would have a negative impact on the open world gameplay. Since players can go wherever they like from the very start of the adventure, the team had to find a way to organize the events of the present day in a coherent way, no matter what path the player chose to follow. Similarly, it had to be possible to discover the events of the past in any order—hence the system of hidden memories, each revealing a fragment of the tragedy from a century earlier. More generally, Aonuma wanted to make it possible for players to finish the game without learning all the ins and outs of the story. *Breath of the Wild* proves revolutionary in this regard, as players are never strictly required to complete the specified missions to make progress in the game. As Aonuma puts it, "If someone goes straight to the end without doing anything else, there are two possibilities: they're either a very good player or slightly deranged. But it's not impossible. That's the way I made the game. It can be fun for fans to challenge each other and see who can finish the game first." And though only the most dedicated of speedrunners would dare to attempt it, players actually can take on Ganon right at the very start of the game, without even taking control of the Divine Beasts first. In that case, of course, the four monsters that control them will be one more obstacle in Link's path. Behind this challenge— which is admittedly of little interest to most players—lies the innovative idea of adapting the adventure to work with everyone's unique way of playing. If the story doesn't interest you, the game will certainly allow you to run right to the ending in a straight line, but you'll miss most of the hidden memories and only get a vague idea of what *Breath of the Wild*'s story is all about. In hindsight, we can only tip our hats to Nintendo's audacious decision to make exploring 100% of the game's content worthwhile by providing a sufficiently attractive reward to motivate players to go hunting for every single mystery hidden throughout the world. This approach has also been well-received by gamers who love a challenge, judging by the number of speedrunners who have attempted the seemingly impossible feat of finishing the game in less than two hours!

A NARRATIVE BLACKOUT THAT LAUNCHED A THOUSAND WILD PREDICTIONS

While Nintendo's media blackout strategy was an effective way to build excitement around the game's release without spoiling any surprises about its content, it also encouraged some fairly wild speculation about *Breath of the Wild*'s storyline. Even the tiniest new clue appearing in images or videos on the Web immediately sent fans into hysterics, throwing out all kinds of imaginative interpretations about the game's story and its place in the overall timeline. Now that the dust has settled, it's worth a moment of our time to look back at how some of these theories got started and to test their plausibility.

The first hint from Nintendo about the setting of this new episode—and indeed, the only thing that fans could be sure of for many long months—was that the world of *Breath of the Wild* had fallen into chaos and devastation. While the first videos showed us natural landscapes that were still lush and green, though also infested with potentially dangerous creatures, we saw no signs of life except for a few animals, perhaps implying that only the wildlife had managed to survive in this untamed countryside. The Temple of Time, an iconic symbol of the Hyrule Sacred Realm, appeared in an August 2016 video as an abandoned pile of rubble, with no indication of how it had come to be in this ruined state. As for the Master Sword, which also appeared in the same trailer, it seemed likely to play a major role in the story, having waited an eternity for the chosen one to appear and draw it from its pedestal. For fans of the series, these images contributed to a vision of a kingdom that had suffered a terrible catastrophe and was patiently waiting to rise up once again. Going further, some even tried to explain the legendary sword's degraded condition by the fact that it was not inside the Temple of Time, which was supposed to protect it from the passing years, but hidden in the forest. While Ganon had made sure to destroy the Temple of Time before the hero could get there, someone had still managed to get away with the precious sword, which was now hidden from the evil one's sight. These initial interpretations seemed to hold up well enough, but we still knew very little about the narrative details of *Breath of the Wild*.

Still refusing to give away the mystery behind the catastrophe that had left Hyrule in this sorry state, the trailers released after August 2016 revealed only that our hero had awakened after sleeping for more than a century. This raised many questions of its own and launched a whole new round of theories. In the end, fans would have to wait until the last few weeks before the game was released for a final round of clues to enliven the debate—and sow discord among fans as to the game's place in the *Zelda* chronology.

THE DELICATE QUESTION OF THE TIMELINE

The first points of disagreement about the setting of *Breath of the Wild* arose in the summer of 2016, with the release of a trailer containing certain unexpected elements. The video in question established a surprising parallel between *Breath of the Wild* and another game in the series, revealing the presence of a tribe that players had first discovered in *The Wind Waker*: the Koroks. Directly descended from the Kokiri tribe who live in the forest regions of *Ocarina of Time*, as explained in the official encyclopedia *Hyrule Historia*, the Koroks are little creatures who somewhat resemble woodland spirits, similar to the Kodama from the Studio Ghibli film *Princess Mononoke*. Visually, the Koroks are no larger than young human children, and their faces are always masked by tree leaves, with different individuals wearing different types of leaves. Before the game was released, learning that this tribe would be present in *Breath of the Wild* mainly served to hint at where this episode would fit in to the overall timeline of the series. In *The Wind Waker*, the former kingdom of Hyrule had sunk to the bottom of the ocean, and the dilapidated state of the new Hyrule seen in *Breath of the Wild* seemed compatible with the idea of a world that had disappeared beneath the waves for many years. On the other hand, another set of theories argued that the visible scars left on the world proved that it had suffered under Ganon's cruelty, which would place the game in the timeline in which Hyrule had fallen into decline after the Hero of Time was defeated in *Ocarina of Time*. According to these theories, the world had become hostile and wild after centuries of abandonment. Since the ocean-world era of *The Wind Waker* is set in the aftermath of the Hero of Time's victory, it is incompatible with the theory of a Hyrule in decline after Link's defeat.

Not until December 2016, just three months before *Breath of the Wild* was released, were fans treated to the first trailer containing specific elements tied to the game's storyline. It began with a painting depicting the legend of ancient times, placed alongside events from the game as if to suggest that history was bound to repeat itself. Then, viewers finally got a clear look at members of the tribes that had long defined the franchise: Zoras, Gorons, Gerudos... and most importantly, the Ritos, whose presence in *Breath of the Wild* defied everyone's expectations. First introduced in *The Wind Waker*, the Ritos people were one tribe that fans weren't expecting to see in this episode, even if the Koroks' presence in the game had at least raised it as a possibility. But why exactly was this such a surprise?

According to the official history in *Hyrule Historia*, the Ritos are the direct descendants of the Zora people, their appearance having evolved considerably during the ocean era. Originally somewhat similar to dolphins, these marine creatures eventually traded in their gills for birds' beaks, and even sprouted wings once they reached adulthood. And yet, the trailer for *Breath of the Wild* also showed glimpses of a member of the Zora tribe. In other words, the game would include at least one representative of both tribes, co-existing in the same world—in direct contradiction to the explanations in the official encyclopedia. Naturally, everyone had their own hypothesis to share. Perhaps this game would feature a new timeline in which the Zora people had not completely transformed. Or maybe the Ritos in *Breath of the Wild* came from different origins than those in *The Wind Waker*. The truth was finally revealed by producer Eiji Aonuma himself, who explained in an interview that *Breath of the Wild* had no direct link with *The Wind Waker*—implying that the theory placing the new game in the same timeline as the Hero of the Wind was untenable and that it would instead take place in the timeline following Ganon's defeat of the Hero of Time. Therefore, if we commit to following the official overall timeline of the series, this game was meant to show us what happened to the kingdom of Hyrule after Link failed to stop Ganon in *Ocarina of Time*.

Whether the Hero of Time had survived his defeat or whether he had been brought back to life by powerful Sheikah technology, *Breath of the Wild*'s place in the overall timeline was finally becoming clearer. In addition, most fans were more attached to *Ocarina of Time* than to *The Wind Waker* and were therefore reassured by this news. More importantly, though, they were impatient to see how this title—which represented a sort of missing link, if you will, between *Ocarina of Time* and *A Link to the Past*—would help to fill in the timeline of Hyrule's decline by adding its own piece to the puzzle. Of all the debates that arose during the long period of uncertainty about the story that preceded the game's release, this was certainly the fiercest, which is why we chose to make room for it in our discussion.

In light of these different factors, everyone is free to decide for themselves what they think of the creators' decision to impose a specific chronology on the series. In fact, there were probably also certain differences of opinion on this point even within Nintendo, as indirectly implied by a handful of contradictions in the official timeline itself. So perhaps the timeline was nothing more than a simple gimmick—a concession to fans who had loudly demanded it, but with no essential impact on the games that came along afterwards. Still, the franchise does have a certain number of constant features that any *Zelda* worthy of the name is required to include. Even more iconic than the trinity of goddesses and the golden triangles, the eternal villain Ganon would seem to be the single most unchanging element in the saga. Nintendo has clearly indicated that it is always the same opponent that players have been asked to confront throughout the ages and even went so far as to explain his origins in *Skyward Sword*. At the end of this episode, which marks the very start of the official timeline, the main villain—known simply as Demise—is sealed away in the legendary sword. But the moment of peace we see at the end of the game is only an illusion; in fact, it marks the beginning of the cursed cycle seen in chronologically later episodes, in which The Evil is perpetually reincarnated through the character of Ganondorf Dragmire. Relentlessly pursuing the heirs of the goddess Hylia and the soul of the hero, starting with the events of *Ocarina of Time*, the king of the Gerudo tribe also acquires his beast form for the first time in that game when he comes into contact with the Triforce. He thus becomes the demon king Ganon, a hideous and demonic creature utterly devoid of humanity. Ironically, it is ultimately through Ganon that the official chronology achieves a certain degree of cohesion, since nothing can ever stop him from eventually being resurrected.

A FOCUS ON THE NATURAL WORLD

While the original inspiration to make *Breath of the Wild* a vast world that players could explore without limits was largely due to director Hidemaro Fujibayashi, the idea of giving the natural world a central place in the adventure was one of producer Eiji Aonuma's top recommendations from the beginning. In a March 2017 interview with the French site *Gameblog.fr*, Aonuma talks about where he got this urge to pay tribute to nature itself and why the natural world was such a source of fascination for him. He explains that the contrast he felt when leaving the countryside in Nagano prefecture to go to work in a big city made him realize how much he missed nature. As a child, constantly surrounded by snow-covered mountains, he had no idea how lucky he was. Only after becoming an adult and suddenly finding himself deprived of the natural environment in which he had grown up, did Aonuma realize how much he missed it. Since then, he regularly hops on his motorbike and heads to the top of a mountain to contemplate the Sea of Japan, bringing him feelings of joy and fulfillment that he hoped to reproduce in *Breath of the Wild*. And indeed, there's no shortage of opportunities in this game to enjoy breathtaking panoramic views of a world whose topography is a constant invitation to explore every nook and cranny to see what secrets we'll stumble upon next.

The silence at the end of the world

We don't realize how much we care about something until it's gone. This is the message that comes through when we look out over the world of *Breath of the Wild*, so badly disfigured after Ganon's victory over the armies of Hyrule that we soon find ourselves wondering what's really left of the kingdom after the tragedy. Similar to a post-apocalyptic landscape, the world of the game has experienced a dramatic upheaval, the effects of which are still being felt a century later. The failure of Link and the four other Champions has plunged Hyrule into chaos, life has given way to death, and the Calamity's dark shadow reaches far beyond the castle to the furthest corners of the kingdom. After such an incredible catastrophe, players naturally fear the worst and halfway expect to discover a world completely devoid of life. But rather than going to quite such discouraging extremes, the creators of the game chose to highlight the absence of life by presenting traces of a natural world and a population that are just waiting for a chance to be reborn. Not only did some people survive the tragedy, but even those who were lost still live on through their descendants. Fully aware of their own difficult situation, the remaining populations have gathered in small villages or simple roadside way stations to await the day when they can return to their homes in regions of the kingdom that are currently too hostile to venture into. After all, there is an entire abandoned world to rebuild out there, but everyone knows that it would be pointless to try anything until Hyrule Castle is freed from the Calamity's clutches. Quite unlike the other episodes of the series, then, the NPCs in *Breath of the Wild* express a sense of real sadness. Only *Majora's Mask*, already an outlier in the series due to its end-of-the-world atmosphere, reflected this sort of depressive fatalism in the words and attitudes of its NPCs. That tone was justified by the fact that everyone was aware of the impending chaos—a sense of trauma that grew all the more intense with each tick of the fateful countdown. After all, unless the hero could manage to reverse its fate, the world of Termina had just three days left before the moon, its leering face drawing closer by the hour, would crash into the planet and destroy it.

The characters in *Breath of the Wild* are survivors, then, but survivors who fear that their fate has already been sealed. They realize that they're powerless against the Guardians and are afraid of being snatched up by monsters or members of the Yiga clan whenever they venture outside. On certain cursed nights, the dark omen known as the blood moon appears to awaken evil creatures from the grave as the cycle of death grows ever stronger, leaving little hope for life to triumph in the end. As if to confirm the danger faced by anyone who dares to set foot outside their villages, it's not unusual to run into NPCs asking for help when they are harassed by monsters much more powerful than them. It is then up to us to save them by slaying their tormentors—or leave them to fend for themselves, since these random encounters are of course strictly optional.

When the adventure first begins and we spend the first few hours of the game without seeing anyone but an old hermit in exile who turns out to be a ghost from the past, it's easy to believe that the world has been so utterly ravaged that we may never meet another living soul who we can talk to. Later on, even after our discovery of different communities established throughout the kingdom has reassured us that we're not completely alone after all, a sense of extreme loneliness still pervades most of our time with the game. This feeling is quite similar to what we experience when playing as Wander, the vulnerable hero who faces his destiny alone in Fumito Ueda's masterpiece *Shadow of the Colossus*, which initially came out in October 2005 for the PlayStation 2. The sense of melancholy in this game is so strong, as we wander the desolate landscape with only our loyal steed to accompany us, that solitude itself becomes a palpable presence to which we have to adapt. Similarly, *Breath of the Wild* is the only episode of the *Zelda* series in which Link spends so much time cut off from any form of civilization. His only interactions are brief and fleeting and, just as in *Shadow of the Colossus*, the challenges he faces have something mystical about them. At many different points in the game, Link's wanderings lead him to various unusual challenges dictated in a guttural voice by some god or higher creature whose identity is unknown to him. And just like Wander, who has no choice but to follow the commands of the voice that orders him to take down these imposing colossi one by one, Link knows that he must overcome these trials to improve his chances of completing his quest. Whether he is required to find his way out of a vast labyrinth, carry an orb along a winding path strewn with obstacles, or survive on a deserted island with no equipment, the purpose of each of these trials is to confront Link with a unique situation that is sharply distinguished from the rest of the game. We have a sense of having reached the very edges of the world, in places where no one is meant to venture, requiring Link to prove that he does deserve to be there. It seems clear that Eiji Aonuma, who has spoken of his friendship with Fumito Ueda and his appreciation for the games produced by Team ICO (*ICO*, *Shadow of the Colossus*, *The Last Guardian*), wanted to establish a common thread between these different worlds through this feeling of solitude and the need to climb and explore every part of the environment in order to survive in *Breath of Wild*. Going further with these parallels, the stages of the game where Link approaches the Divine Beasts recall the scenes where Wander climbs the colossi; in both cases, the player is keenly aware of how vulnerable they are in the presence of these beings, which could crush them without batting an eye.

REVEALING THE RADIANCE OF THE NATURAL WORLD

If the world of *Breath of the Wild* had been limited to dark visions of a post-apocalyptic Hyrule completely devastated by war, it would have lacked the dreamlike quality that ultimately makes it so fascinating. In reality, though, all of the negative and deadly elements are counterbalanced by the shimmering beauty of a natural world that is gradually reclaiming its place. While the surviving humanoid populations stay hidden away in fear of the dangers that swirl and swarm around them, wild animals continue to venture into the Guardians' territory to keep on living as best they can. Similarly, lush green landscapes contrast with the desolate scenes that become more and more frequent as we approach the lair where the Calamity lies in wait. Groups of wild animals explore the world freely, and their spontaneous reactions help make the world feel more realistic and alive. For example, wolves always travel in packs, and they are quick to attack Link if he gets too close to their territory— but just as quick to run away if he manages to kill one of them. The other ferocious animals that he meets as he wanders through the forests, mountains, or vast plains of Hyrule also show similar behavior. From fierce predators to skittish game animals, all of these creatures seem to be living their own lives, and while the foxes, caribou, herons, and boars we encounter are easy prey to keep us well-stocked with meat, there's nothing forcing us to stir up trouble in this natural environment that doesn't wish us any harm. In fact, some players might even feel a bit guilty for hunting these virtual creatures, without which our adventure would be almost unbearably lonely; since wild nature and the creatures that live within it are what bring this devastated world to life, why would we want to hurt them?

It's hard to guess at exactly what point in the process the *Breath of the Wild* team decided to accord such a central role to Hyrule's wildlife, which is so captivating and so similar to the animals we know from our own world. But one thing is clear: the presence of all these animals that bolt away at our slightest abrupt movement is what makes exploring the world such an enjoyable experience. Probably because these fundamentally wild creatures generally do their best to stay out of sight, the designers had the brilliant idea to let players tame them in a totally innovative way that stands in sharp contrast to how this process normally works in video games. Halfway between wild predators and the dogs and other pets that we can interact with at the trading posts, we also find wild horses in *Breath of the Wild* that we can try to capture. One glance at these noble creatures is enough to see how much work the team put into making these animals as realistic as anything else in the game. Hidden in the high grass and almost holding our breath with excitement, we can observe these horses animated with an incredible level of skill, matched only by the outstanding visual design that gives the whole game the look of an animated film. Everything about the animation of these creatures reflects their wild and fiery spirit, encouraging us to carefully creep up close enough to grab hold of one and try to tame it. With enough tenacity, patience, and stamina, our insistence on approaching them will be rewarded... after a few moments of fierce bucking and rearing. Suddenly finding ourselves clinging desperately to the back of a wild horse, with just a handful of its mane to control it when the animal has no interest in obeying our directions, provides a moment of pure enchantment. Like the Little Prince taming his fox in Saint-Exupéry's classic tale, we learn to establish ties with our new friend by paying attention to its reactions and praising it every time it seems to respond to our commands. In the game as in real life, rewarding the horse by patting it at the right moment to communicate our feelings wordlessly is the only way to form a connection to the animal that could become our most faithful steed. Only after we have guided it to the nearest stable can the horse acquire a saddle, bridle, and a name—and even after that, you must continue the work of taming it until your bond is at its maximum level if you want your horse to follow your every command. Since every horse has its own unique temperament and abilities, certain individuals may prove more restive, faster, or more resilient than others. The only flaw in this otherwise realistic approach lies in the fact that painted horses (with white and dark pinto spotting) are easier to mount than others, although that doesn't stop them from rearing up or throwing us off if we're too rough with them.

While it's true that many games before it have done a fine job of including horses as privileged companions for open world adventurers (*Red Dead Redemption*, *The Witcher 3*, *Assassin's Creed*, *Shadow of the Colossus*), *Breath of the Wild* is the first to assign them such central importance. However, despite the impressive level of attention paid to their design and behavior in the game, this search for absolute realism sometimes goes against the habits that players have developed for making their way through the game. For example, it is impossible to teleport with a horse, so our steed has to get to us the long way when we whistle to summon it—and only if the landscape allows it. Similarly, we have to be at a stable to hop in the saddle of one of our five horses, adding a further constraint to our dreams of galloping through the wild countryside at breakneck speed. In addition, there's always a certain risk of losing our equine companion in altercations between mounted combatants, since Bokoblins are also perfectly capable of wielding bows and melee weapons on the backs of wild horses. Arrows that miss their target can therefore easily kill our horse if we're not careful. Of course, the game also provides a trick to avoid losing a steed forever to such twists of fate, but it is rare to see a game go this far in its treatment of horses, which are too often reduced to little more than a means of transportation. In *Breath of the Wild*, the pleasure of riding is emphasized to such an extent that the game allows us to ride bareback, climb into the saddle in four different ways, and execute real dressage movements (lateral movements and pseudo-piaffes) to squirm through even the tightest spots. If players choose to shoot a bow from horseback, they'll have to do it with no aim assistance... and two-handed swords have a better chance of hitting their target or knocking a mounted enemy out of the saddle... and of course, we can also steal that enemy's horse for ourselves once they're down on the ground. The ultimate proof that the *Breath of the Wild* is made of true lovers of the "noblest conquest of man" is that they even thought to punish less scrupulous players who whip their horses too much by unceremoniously disqualifying them from the mounted obstacle course, one of the most technical minigames in the adventure!

And while we're at it, why limit the fun to just riding horses? Amazingly enough, the kinds of activities that are normally banned in video games are perfectly possible in *Breath of the Wild*. For example, whether we choose a sneaky approach or simply wait for just the right moment to jump on a wild animal as it runs up to attack us, there's nothing stopping us from climbing onto any animal's back in a daring attempt at taming it. Whether we succeed depends on how much stamina we've managed to accumulate first. What could be more exhilarating than galloping through the woods on the back of a doe, a buck, or even a bear, knowing that the animal could easily escape from our control at any moment? The game offers so much freedom in this regard that it almost feels frustrating to discover that we can't ride on absolutely any animal in the game—a shame, since cows and caribou would also have made for impressive and heroic steeds. On the other hand, the game does allow us to hop onto a Sand Seal's back to cruise long distances in the desert and even to briefly mount a Lynel, one of the mighty centaurs that can only be brought down with a faceful of arrows. The *Zelda* series has taken us to many magical and dreamlike places over the years, both realistic and fantastic, so it's no surprise to find that *Breath of the Wild* also offers a thousand different ways to be delighted and amazed.

REALISM AND MYSTICISM

One of the most surprising realizations that we come to while playing *Breath of the Wild* is that nearly all of the game's content seems to have been designed in advance to be optional. As a result, it would be easy to finish the main quest while ignoring a staggering number of hidden secrets. Unless we spend a hundred hours or so exploring the vast world of Hyrule, there is always something new to discover, some new detail that we missed before and might only discover by chance in the course of our long wanderings. It is here that the game willingly slips into mysticism, offering quests that aren't really quests, but simply additional reasons to enjoy the game's many astounding secrets. In *Breath of the Wild*, for example, we find great fairies made up like French noblewomen of the Enlightenment era, in an even more bizarre style than the fairies in *Ocarina of Time* who were as unsettling to the player as they were to our unfortunate hero. We also find a certain number of legendary creatures that even the natives of Hyrule consider to be little more than folk tales, like the glowing rabbits known as Blupees—said to bring wealth and good luck. Only the luckiest players will catch a glimpse of their leader, Alpha, a creature that represents the ultimate nature spirit and recalls the visual style of the film *Princess Mononoke* by Studio Ghibli. This mystical horse-like creature can only be discovered in the light of a green glow found high on Satori Mountain; sometimes known as the Sage or the Lord of the Mountain, it takes the form of a majestic four-legged being that Link can ride, but that offers no other reward except the joy of discovering it. And because nothing is ever entirely as it seems in *Breath of the Wild*, Nintendo has hinted that this supernatural creature actually symbolizes the late Satoru Iwata, the former CEO of Nintendo, as a hidden tribute to the wise man after whom Satori Mountain is said to be named.

The game includes a number of startlingly dreamlike sequences like these and also offers more adventuresome players the privilege of taming other exceptional mounts—like the ones said to have belonged to Zelda or to Ganon himself or the skeleton horse that melts away in the light of the sun, leaving nothing behind but a vague memory of having witnessed some sort of witchcraft. There is also plenty of magic to be found in the Korok Forest, home of the most timid creatures in the entire *Zelda* saga, whom we first met in *The Wind Waker* and who are scattered throughout the world here, though carefully hidden from view. There's surely no longer quest in the history of video games than Link's pursuit of the nine hundred Koroks hiding in *Breath of the Wild*, given the enormous size of the world. But that's precisely what makes this extraordinary challenge so difficult to resist. Faithfully watching over the precious legendary sword, the venerable Great Deku Tree, who was Link's first guide in *Ocarina of Time*, also appears here as the other great figure of the Korok Forest, speaking to our hero with the sadness of an old master who realizes that his protégé has lost all memory of him. After his hundred-year slumber, Link had forgotten that the Great Deku Tree even existed until it began to recite the tale of the events that came before.

Of all the strange creatures to be discovered in *Breath of the Wild*, the most thrilling stories are of unreal encounters with three legendary dragons who almost always appear just when we least expect to see them. While any other title would have made these enormous creatures the focus of carefully scripted events, *Breath of the Wild* chooses to keep everything about them a complete secret and leaves it entirely to us to solve this mystery in our own way. It's up to the player to discover that these dragons exist and that it's possible to approach them and to learn what role they may have to play; until then, our only clues are a characteristic melody and the occasional unusual updraft.

Since no contextual action appears to help us figure out what to do, the feat of detaching even a single scale from their bodies requires a carefully planned and executed maneuver. It's in this type of situation, where the player seeks help but receives none, that they can truly savor the value of their achievements.

Seeing the world around us living and changing on its own, without the slightest need for any action on our part, is one of *Breath of the Wild*'s most remarkable accomplishments. Juxtaposing chaos and death with the emergence of a vibrant natural world gradually returning to life, the game environment makes us aware of our own fragility in the face of forces raging out of control or defying all comprehension. The world is so full of mysteries that it's virtually impossible to get from one point to another without unconsciously deviating from our chosen route to check out yet another unexpected element that's caught our attention. Playing *Breath of the Wild* is not so much about pursuing a specific quest as it is about exploring for the sheer pleasure of discovery, letting our wandering eyes lead us from one surprise to the next—and if that means taking a little longer (or a lot longer) to get where we're going, then so be it.

THE MUSIC OF *ZELDA*: FROM TRADITION TO IMMERSION

BREAKING OLD HABITS

As bold and unique in its musical choices as in every other respect, *Breath of the Wild* also breaks with the tradition of earlier *Zelda* games by including new and unexpected compositions based more on the immediate context than on our overall progression in the adventure. This break with the other OSTs (original soundtracks) in the series is reflected in the near-total absence of musical themes associated with specific stages in the development of the story, and the themes we do hear are integrated much more discreetly than usual. Like other games that focus more on establishing an effective atmosphere than on pure musical entertainment (and here we can again highlight the similarities with *Shadow of the Colossus*), *Breath of the Wild* does not treat its music as an end in itself. In other words, it seems that the sound designers never considered developing the game's OST as a simple succession of epic compositions that would stay stuck in our heads at the end of every gaming session. Instead, the choices made here are oriented more toward treating the soundtrack as just one more way to help structure the player's adventure, in contrast to its usual role as a separate component that can be completely dissociated from what's happening on screen. For decades, video games have been using music to guide the player's progression to the beat of scripted events, alternating between a certain number of zones with different themes symbolized by musical compositions that sometimes stay with us long after we've forgotten all about the levels themselves. The choices made in *Breath of the Wild* go in precisely the opposite direction, and we sense the team's desire to find a musical compromise that supports the in-game action without getting in its way. So while we do encounter a few major themes in this episode, they only appear on certain rare occasions and almost always take a back seat to the action unfolding on-screen.

These changes may surprise and unsettle certain longtime fans of the series who expect to hear memorable tunes accompanying their every move in the game, just as they almost always have throughout the history of the franchise. Of course, the last few trailers for *Breath of the Wild* were fairly misleading on this point, implying that the new episode would be filled with epic themes—a far cry from what actually wound up in the game. In fact, for most of the time that Link spends wandering the great outdoors, what mainly stands out is the conspicuous lack of musical accompaniment. Instead, we hear only the ambient sounds of nature unless something disrupts our travels. The soundtrack of *Breath of the Wild* is completely dynamic, adapting to the changing contexts of each individual play session; if enemies suddenly appear, the surrounding calm is quickly replaced by a musical frenzy that continues until the danger has passed. Always perfectly aligned with what's happening in the game, the sound design generally lets nature express itself through the chirping of birds, the rustling of leaves carried along by the wind, or the cries of wild animals. In light of everything discussed earlier about the role of nature in *Breath of the Wild*, we can see how important the decision to opt for a calm, realistic and natural atmosphere turns out to be for the overall believability of the experience. Listening carefully for the slightest unexpected sound, players quickly learn the importance of moving gently and quietly themselves in order to blend into their environment. Ultimately, maintaining this overall silence is the only way to take full advantage of the subtle noises that surround us, while also making us aware of the solitary nature of our immense quest. And when an aggressive musical theme suddenly rings out to warn us of approaching danger, that abrupt signal reminds us to pull ourselves together and be exceptionally vigilant.

In the same way, the music acts as a guide, informing players when they're approaching a stable or close to Kass, the accordion-playing Ritos, by means of a specific melody indicating that one of these points of interest is nearby.

Besides collecting visual information to help them get their bearings, players can also use their hearing to find their way.

In short, we feel as though the game were trying to awaken all of our senses even as Link learns to rely on his, teaching us to survive by our wits without falling back on the endless tutorial tips that weigh down most modern games. In that sense, hearing the sounds of the world around us turns out to be at least as important as our view of our immediate surroundings, even if our perception of those sounds is usually instinctive and unconscious.

Paradoxically, then, the rhythmic themes that we missed at the start of the game suddenly feel more surprising once our ears have started getting used to these ambient sounds. Whether or not we agree with this approach, which seems to delegate the music to a somewhat secondary role, there's no denying that the overall form of *Breath of the Wild* lends itself well to the idea of putting environmental sounds in the foreground. At the same time, we experience each new piece of music that we encounter in a much different way than we would have if the OST had followed a more traditional blueprint. Whether they're completely new or recall other themes we've heard in the past, these pieces often surprise us with their choice of instrumentation. In a behind-the-scenes video about the game's development process, audio director Hajime Wakai explains that most of the music in *Breath of the Wild* consists of piano compositions intended to reinforce the game's environmental sounds. The team quickly decided to focus more on ambient sounds than on music in order to increase the realism of Hyrule's landscapes and environments. We should also note that the score players hear during exploration phases, replaying the same notes on the piano, is not associated with any specific location. Besides being a better fit for the title, this approach turned out to work very well with the choice of piano as the main instrument, even though this was the first time the piano had been used in developing the music for a *Zelda* game. As players make their way through the game, the result is highly refreshing, adding a new touch of color to old melodies we've known for years—as if we were hearing these familiar tunes in distant memories, like fragments of a forgotten era with no hope of recovering their long-lost magic, but still there to underline the events of the story.

The choice of piano thus joins the many other aspects of *Breath of the Wild* that distinguish it so sharply from its predecessors. Combined with the Japanese folk instruments used extensively in most of the compositions heard in-game, the soundtrack takes on a unique, almost mystical aspect that immediately banishes any feeling of "musical déjà vu". This is why certain pieces, like the one that announces the arrival of a legendary dragon, are immediately recognizable from the first few notes alone, even though they're not based on any particularly striking melodies. And although they're quite surprising at first, the pieces that Kass plays on the accordion are also among the most exciting musical discoveries in the game. Because they are intimately tied to the ancient legends and shrine puzzles recounted by this wandering troubadour, these accordion tunes affect us deeply by offering sounds of the past that further reinforce the nostalgic aspect of these scenes. As a result, much like the piano or traditional Japanese folk instruments heard elsewhere, the accordion is an unusual choice that is both evocative and effective.

In the same spirit, familiar *Zelda* themes are handled in an extremely innovative way, with such fundamental changes to their basic tone that they are almost unrecognizable at times. For example, the Kakariko Village theme is utterly transformed by the predominance of traditional Asian sounds. This is also the case for the main theme of the series, which opens with a simple sequence of notes like falling flower petals before the piece takes a more epic turn, in perfect harmony with the sublime natural scenes that make the game so inspiring to explore. In another part of the game, the music that plays as we watch the legend of ten thousand years ago unfold as an animated painting recalls the series theme once heard in the introduction to *A Link to the Past*, even incorporating a chorus of singers at the end to accentuate the grandiose nature of the piece. As for the Lost Woods, they are now scored with a sort of intoxicating litany that only strengthens our feeling of being completely lost, disoriented, and wandering hopelessly in circles. Elsewhere, fans of *The Wind Waker* will easily recognize the Ritos Village melody, reworked to make it more nostalgic and less lively than the original. *Breath of the Wild* also features a deeply oppressive Hyrule Castle theme that wouldn't sound out of place in an OST from the *Castlevania* series, so powerfully does it emphasize Calamity Ganon's utter domination of the place that was once the Sacred Realm's greatest stronghold. It also incorporates a number of iconic melodies from the saga, including the Hyrule Castle melody, the main series theme, and both Zelda's and Ganon's themes. Finally, the shrine theme reprises the one used in the first *Zelda* game and in *A Link to the Past*, while adding a more mystical sound. The echo effects used in this track make it sound like it's emerging from beyond the mists of time, again recalling the saga's rich musical heritage.

To set the right tone, the audio director also insisted on careful treatment of even the most commonplace sounds; for example, considerable work was needed to ensure the authenticity of the wide variety of footstep sounds. In addition, because the various themes are noticeably different at night than during the day, it was also important to make sure that the musical atmosphere remained appropriate for different in-game situations even with the added touch of quiet mystery that's typical of the nighttime melodies. Hajime Wakai adds that nothing was left to chance—a special sound effect was even created by squishing a finger into wet cloth to depict the sound of a Bokoblin picking its nose! Beyond this specific anecdote, this kind of detail reveals how committed the sound effects team was to coming up with imaginative ways to make the game more immersive. In an interview with the *IGN* website, producer Eiji Aonuma recounts another example of this type, explaining how an animal designer and a programmer focused on synchronizing the rhythm of horses' hoof sounds with the associated animations. Few titles go this far just to make the player's experience a little bit more enjoyable by zeroing in on tiny details like these.

Passing the torch

If the soundtrack for *Breath of the Wild* was unlike any before it, the reason might be that the composers behind it were relatively new to the saga. Having been an essential part of the *Super Mario Bros.* and *The Legend of Zelda* series for many years, self-taught composer Koji Kondo had passed the torch to a new generation of artists on the *Zelda* franchise after *Ocarina of Time* was released in 1998, moving to a new role as musical supervisor. Manaka Kataoka and Yasuaki Iwata thus found themselves in charge of the sounds of *Breath of the Wild*. Building on her experience on *The Legend of Zelda: Spirit Tracks*, a handheld episode mainly remembered for its exhilarating main theme, composer Manaka Kataoka also helped to design the music for *Super Smash Bros. for Wii U, Animal Crossing: New Leaf* and *City Folk*, and perhaps most surprisingly, *Wii Fit*. As for Yasuaki Iwata, he had previously been entrusted with the original soundtracks for *Super Mario 3D World* and *Mario Kart 8* before also joining *Super Smash Bros. for Wii U*. With *Breath of the Wild*, the duo delivered the most groundbreaking musical experience since the beginning of the series, bringing a refreshing artistic direction to the series that we hope to hear more of in later installments.

The end of the silent era

Determined to stop at nothing in its dramatic break with tradition, the new *Zelda* game gave voices to its beloved characters for the very first time, marking the end of an uninterrupted succession of episodes that had done without voices. As the main protagonist, however, Link has to remain neutral so that every player can identify with him—making him the only major character who doesn't speak in the new game. Adding voices was a big change that carried certain risks for Nintendo, and it wanted to be sure not to upset fans who were naturally concerned about hearing these iconic figures speak for the first time. Under these conditions, it wasn't surprising when Patricia Summersett, the voice actress who portrayed the English version of Zelda, revealed in an interview with the teen girls' site *Sweety High* that she had experienced a mix of incredible pressure and excitement in the year leading up to the announcement that the game would use voice actors. But players would have to wait for update 1.2.0 in May 2017 before *Breath of the Wild* finally allowed them to change voices on the fly without affecting the subtitle or user-interface languages. This update provided an excellent way to compare the effectiveness of the voices provided for each character in the nine different voice languages, including English and Japanese. In the end, those who feared that adding voices would have a negative impact on the game were reassured to discover that only the most important scenes in the adventure were actually voiced and that the vast majority of dialogues were still as silent as ever.

ZELDA

THE HISTORY OF A LEGENDARY SAGA
VOLUME 2: BREATH OF THE WILD

CHAPTER III

DECRYPTION

AVING looked at the process by which *Breath of the Wild* was created and explored the most symbolic aspects of its narrative universe, it's time to take our discussion a little further by casting a critical eye on the design decisions implemented in the game. We first turn to the inevitable question of the title's technical shortcomings, caught as it is between two console generations and representing both the swan song of one console at the end of its life cycle and the baptism by fire of a new one just taking flight. To what extent did the decision to port *Breath of the Wild* to the Switch at such a late stage in its development have a negative impact on a game that was originally designed for the Wii U? We also take a closer look at what an important development the open world formula has turned out to be for the *Zelda* franchise. How did the game manage to so effectively incorporate the lessons learned from other games that indirectly laid the groundwork for its unique take on the open world genre, leading to the impressive results discussed in the previous chapter? This question relates directly to the designers' choice to rethink the very foundations of the series' classic gameplay, creating a new kind of *Zelda* that invites us to learn how to play all over again with an emphasis on creativity. How dangerous was it to risk upsetting hardcore fans of old-school dungeon crawling and other fans with a near-religious attachment to the many gameplay elements that had defined the series from the beginning? Naturally, we'll also look at how players themselves put the title through its paces, testing the well-oiled machine by venturing well beyond the developers' original intentions.

We will also examine how players' experience of the game is affected by the decision to take open-ended gameplay to its logical limit, while also considering the pros and cons of a gameplay system that's much more realistic and demanding than in earlier installments. We'll then try to determine what makes the hero of *Breath of the Wild* fundamentally different from the other incarnations of Link we've encountered in the series and highlight some ways in which the game chooses to break the fourth wall. Finally, we'll take a hard look at how well the developers kept their original promises and identify some elements that could have been added or improved upon to make *Breath of the Wild* even more effective in its reimagining of the franchise.

GENERATION GAP

Throughout the history of the series (except for the episodes released for handheld consoles), the release of a new *Zelda* game has always been perceived as a major event. Only the biggest names in the world of video games can achieve this level of anticipation—and in *Zelda*'s case, the excitement has often reached truly dizzying heights. Nevertheless, the situation with *Breath of the Wild*, as with *Twilight Princess* a few years earlier, was slightly less clear-cut. Both of these episodes were unusual in that they were released simultaneously on two different consoles. In both cases, releasing two parallel versions ensured a smooth transition between the two console generations, while also making sure that no player would be left behind. So while *The Legend of Zelda: Twilight Princess* brought an end to the GameCube era in 2006 and provided the Wii with a flagship title to give its launch lineup a much-needed boost, the release of *Breath of the Wild* in 2017 symbolized the passing of the torch from the Wii U to the Switch.

At the start of the development process, however, this new *Zelda* episode was intended for release on the Wii U alone—and in fact it was meant for release in 2015, just ahead of the franchise's 30th anniversary. In the end, though, *Breath of the Wild* would be released as a launch title for Nintendo's new console, the Switch, since the original release date turned out to be impossible to achieve. Announced very late in the development process, in the spring of 2016, the decision to port *Breath of the Wild* to the Switch was actually a major selling point for potential buyers of the new console, most of whom might not have been ready to take the plunge without the excitement of a new *Zelda* game to sweeten the deal.

But although releasing the same title on two different machines simultaneously is certainly convenient from consumers' point of view, the decision also quickly raised certain concerns among players. Recall that in 2006, reviewers and fans had criticized the fact that the Wii version of *Twilight Princess* was far too similar to its GameCube equivalent. The Wii version showed no major technical advancements in terms of graphics, and the added ability to control the hero's sword with the Wiimote seemed like little more than a gimmick. In other words, the simultaneous release on two consecutive generations of consoles left recent Wii buyers feeling like they were playing a game from the previous generation.

History repeated itself in 2017, and it is tempting to raise this same criticism once again when we consider how similar the two versions of *Breath of the Wild* are to one another. This wouldn't have been a problem if the game hadn't turned out, in many players' opinions, to be so shaky on the technical side—an issue we will return to later on. And even though no one was really expecting astounding feats of technological prowess from the Switch, many were left with a disappointing overall impression of the game, although its art direction did help to make up for its technical shortcomings. Needless to say, the Wii U version revealed the same limitations—and even more clearly.

It's also interesting to note that there were ultimately even fewer differences between the Switch and Wii U versions of *Breath of the Wild* than there were between the Wii and GameCube versions of *Twilight Princess*. In the latter case, the designers had made the decision to present the Wii game as a mirror image of the GameCube version. Since one of the Wii's unique features was that it allowed players to control Link's sword with the Wiimote, the hero had to suddenly become right-handed (like the majority of the world's population and therefore the majority of gamers), which in turn required an inversion of the game's environments. On GameCube, meanwhile, Link remained a left-handed swordsman, allowing players to rediscover the adventure in a slightly different way. In addition, while the GameCube controller gave players total control over the camera, this was not the case in the Wii version. Though quite rudimentary in 2006, the Wiimote sword controls would be significantly more convincing in 2011's *Skyward Sword* thanks to the Wii Motion Plus accessory, which allowed for much more precise weapon control.

As for *Breath of the Wild*, most of the differences between the two versions were visual in nature. The Switch also offered quicker loading times due to cartridge support and its more powerful audio processor. Perhaps because Nintendo wanted to focus attention on the Switch version, which was technically cleaner and more polished, it took a long time for the press to receive their copies of the Wii U version. In comparative videos and by word of mouth, Wii U players complained of recurring problems with slow and jerky animations due to frequent drops in the game's framerate, excessive aliasing and blurry textures, and, of course, the lower resolution (720p instead of 900p)—all resulting in a less enjoyable game experience than on the Switch. In other words, while *Breath of the Wild* is hardly a technological monster on the new Nintendo console, it easily outclasses its Wii U equivalent, even though the game had initially been designed for exclusive release on the Wii U.

The other reason that buyers of the Wii U game were disappointed was that the Gamepad, which includes an integrated secondary touchscreen, does not provide any relevant functionality in *Breath of the Wild*, whereas some Wii U games (or at least a few, like *ZombiU* and *Nintendo Land*) bend over backwards to find the most innovative ways to use it. In *Breath of the Wild*, the Gamepad could have been used to display the world map, for example (as certain trailers clearly implied that it would), the sub-menu, or even other options that would distinguish it from the Switch version, including touch-based gameplay elements. Instead, the designers decided to offer two identical gameplay experiences and merely provided the option to play in handheld mode on the two secondary screens (the Gamepad on the Wii U and the Switch's handheld screen). But this was not a trivial choice. In fact, it's interesting to note that the decision to port the game to the Switch, after development was already well underway, led to a number of significant changes to the original version.

Producer Eiji Aonuma was certainly in an ideal position to understand the issues involved in developing a game for two platforms at the same time, having faced a similar situation back when he was working as the director of *Twilight Princess*. In a 2017 interview with the website *Gamekult*, he explained that he found that transition more difficult to manage than the one for *Breath of the Wild*, mainly due to his lack of experience at the time in developing two simultaneous versions of a game. But it was the lessons he learned on *Twilight Princess* that helped Aonuma to anticipate what would need to be done in the process of developing *Breath of the Wild* to ensure that both the Switch and Wii U versions would offer the same high-quality experience for the player. For example, the team decided that the Gamepad screen would have to do without its main functionality in the Wii U version in order to align it with the experience provided by the Switch version. Along the same lines, director Hidemaro Fujibayashi admitted that he did not regret having to leave out various touch-based gameplay elements that had originally been planned, because he was concerned that having to look away from the main screen too often would break the player's immersion—a decision that once again served to disavow the core concept of the Wii U.

Originally, however, the plan was to establish a direct analogy between the Sheikah Slate in Link's hands and the Gamepad held by the player. The Sheikah Slate is a constant presence throughout the adventure, and this approach would have made players feel like they were interacting with it directly through the Gamepad, with the images and data on the screen changing to reflect the specific functions they were using. Better yet, the slate was supposed to "talk" to players by reading out the information shown on the second screen through the Gamepad's audio output.

Clearly, the decision to abandon this initial idea wound up having a drastic impact on players' potential enjoyment of this version. Instead of making clever use of the Wii U's much-vaunted capacity for asymmetric gameplay, the older console was forced to humbly make way for its shiny new cousin, the Switch.

Presumably, Nintendo didn't want to let the Wii U version have any advantages that its new console would have to do without, given that *Breath of the Wild* was supposed to be the flagship title for the Switch. At that point, probably the best that this ill-treated "original" version could hope to accomplish was to give a broader range of players a chance to discover the game. In the end, the Wii U—which had been patiently awaiting a chance to welcome its "very own *Zelda*" after a slew of ported versions of earlier episodes—was unceremoniously kicked out of the spotlight by the new Switch for reasons that amounted to little more than a marketing ploy.

It took a while for the Switch version of *Breath of the Wild* to convince potential console buyers to take the plunge, since most players were disappointed by the game's technical shortcomings on what they had hoped would be a more powerful platform. Their reluctance continued even after update 1.1.1 was released on March 31, 2017, to provide improved framerate stability for both versions of the game. In addition, the difference in the graphics quality between games played through the dock (and thus displayed on a TV screen) and in handheld mode (on the Switch's portable screen) soon turned out to be quite significant, with handheld sessions running much more smoothly. This result was both regrettable and highly unexpected for a title that many players had planned to explore exclusively on their big-screen TVs.

Despite all this, *Breath of the Wild*'s technical limitations didn't prevent huge numbers of players from falling in love with the game's vast and exciting content and its obvious qualities in terms of gameplay. Besides, Nintendo had made it clear that the Switch version didn't use anywhere near the full power of the console, since it was essentially a port of a game that had originally been planned for the Wii U. While the development process had focused on a port from one generation to the next that was relatively easy due to the difference in power between the two machines, the new game reflected only a small part of what the Switch would be able to offer once developers had fully mastered its technology. On that note, producer Eiji Aonuma hinted that the Switch would probably have a chance to welcome an all-new episode of *Zelda* in the future— but this time specifically designed for this platform from the beginning and able to make full use of its technological potential and special functionalities like HD Rumble. The only question is: how long will we have to wait?

MASTERING THE OPEN WORLD FORMULA

As soon as players learned that the next *Zelda* title would be based around an open world concept, fans who had been waiting for years for the next episode went through a whole range of emotions. If we had to roughly summarize the overall feeling, perhaps the best way to describe it would be as a nearly-unbearable sense of euphoria weighed down by legitimate doubts about whether Nintendo's wild gamble would actually succeed. What were the chances that the Japanese developer, with its extremely limited experience with the open world formula, would manage to pull it off without inflicting potentially irreparable damage to the series' prestigious image? After all, contrary to Japanese games' well-known reluctance to let players run free in a virtual environment that they are unlikely to ever explore completely, it is Western RPGs that have given open world games their reputation for excellence. So even accepting the basic idea that *Breath of the Wild* would suddenly be able to compete with the masters of the genre on their own turf meant believing in Nintendo's ability to make up for lost time and even propose new ideas that would earn it the right to stand alongside the biggest names in open world game design. Therefore, even the most optimistic fans couldn't help but be a little anxious about how the development team would manage to avoid the pitfalls associated with such an immense challenge.

On the shoulders of giants

But those who doubted Nintendo's creative resources might have been forgetting the many occasions on which the company had already proven its ability to bounce back and surprise everyone just when it had seemed least likely to succeed. For example, simply thinking back to how most of its consoles were designed is enough to remind us that Nintendo is better than anyone at drawing on the core essence of existing technologies to create something completely new. This was true of the Nintendo DS, which reinvented how we played on handheld consoles by incorporating a dual screen, including one screen with ingenious tactile features. To a lesser extent, it was also true of the Nintendo 3DS, which uses an autostereoscopic 3D display to let players enjoy games in three dimensions with no need for 3D glasses. And although it turned out to be a resounding flop, even the Virtual Boy deserves credit for boldly exploring the experimental realm of virtual reality back in 1995.

So it was with much the same mindset that Nintendo decided with *Breath of the Wild* to develop its own take on the open world game as applied to the world of *Zelda*, while also taking a distinctly Japanese approach to the process. Nintendo may have been new at creating open world games, but it had long since mastered the art of studying what works for players and identifying the reasons why. With this in mind, it's easier to understand how this new *Zelda* game was able to achieve the unthinkable: successfully impressing Western audiences simply by taking inspiration from its predecessors, absorbing the lessons learned, and coming up with its own unique spin on the genre. Although the concept of an open world is hardly new anymore, the creative minds at Nintendo have shown that it is still possible to transcend the genre simply by coming to the development process with a desire to offer a new vision of what it can be.

Ultimately, *Breath of the Wild* drew freely from the whole range of Western influences to create something uniquely its own. Whether it's the gigantic towers that Link has to climb to reveal a map of the surrounding area, in a direct reference to the gameplay logic of the *Assassin's Creed* series, or the need to manage food, materials, and resources that has been at the core of Western CRPGs for years, the new *Zelda* clearly didn't mind borrowing from its predecessors in a few fairly obvious ways to build its own gameplay systems. But the creators of *Breath of the Wild* went further by not providing too much detail about the regions surrounding each of the towers that players activate. Whereas most open world games (*Assassin's Creed Syndicate, Horizon: Zero Dawn*) reveal the exact location of various secrets on the map as soon as the conditions to unlock them have been met, the new *Zelda* game only shows us the general topography of the area. It's then up to us to take advantage of the lofty perspective provided by these towers to locate Shrines and other points of interest and then to explore these environments on foot in order to add our own more precise information to the world map. This information may be added automatically, in the case of villages, dungeons, or stables, which immediately appear on the map as soon as we first approach them, or manually, as the player can add as many stamps as they like to plan for their future exploration efforts. What's most incredible here is that the world contains so many mysteries (monsters' lairs, treasures, shrines, towers, Koroks, etc.) that the 100 stamps available for use on the map are not enough to flag everything we might like to take note of manually.

This single example is enough to give us an idea of how well Nintendo has succeeded here at taking a well-established idea and reimagining it in new and unique ways, simply to put a more interesting spin on gameplay concepts that are normally intended to help the player. In *Breath of the Wild*, the towers' role is no longer to simply activate a long checklist of new tasks to be completed on autopilot, sending us mechanically from one checkpoint to another on an overcrowded map. Instead, they give us an overview of the general outlines of the territories we have yet to explore, but never force us to go about it in any specific way—nor, in fact, do players get much in the way of hints at all. In other words, rather than telling players what to do, the game simply suggests certain responses that coincide with what they were already planning to do. At the same time, the absence of any barriers in Hyrule's vast landscape opens up more ways to explore the world of the game; invisible walls will never put a stop to our most creative and adventurous impulses.

Similarly, while the systems for collecting resources and food in *Breath of the Wild* owe much to the CRPG genre, the approach taken here is fairly innovative in that these systems provide one of the only ways to survive in the game's hostile environment. Since Link can no longer regenerate hearts by breaking pots or cutting grass, he now has to collect all kinds of natural food ingredients (fruits, mushrooms, venison) by his own efforts. Eaten raw, these items only provide a minimal boost of life energy, but they offer much greater benefits when cooked—sometimes including special bonuses like resistance to certain extreme weather conditions, increased stamina or stealth, additional hearts, and so on. The strength of these bonus effects increases with the number of different ingredients in a given meal.

While it's true that *Breath of the Wild* was not the first Japanese video game to include tasty dishes like these (already familiar from *Final Fantasy XV* or most games from Vanillaware, including *Odin Sphere* and *Muramasa*), the focus on cooking in the newest *Zelda* game went well beyond anything that players had seen before. Surviving for even a few hours in *Breath of the Wild* without gathering a minimal supply of cooked meals is a significant challenge, forcing the player to quickly test out the different possible combinations to discover their various effects (an increase in the number of hearts restored, a temporary boost to the stamina wheel, resistance to heat or cold, etc.). The designers even went so far as to add a special "censored" visual effect for questionable dishes resulting from inappropriate mixtures of ingredients, reflecting the element of chance inherent in every attempt at cooking. It's up to the user to empirically test the different possible combinations. And just finding a pot isn't always enough to prepare a dish; the player may also need to learn how to light the fire to heat it when no torches or fire arrows are available, perhaps by striking a metal blade on bit of flint over a pile of firewood to produce the spark that sets the wood aflame. The YouTuber known as BeardBear posted a video to his channel demonstrating no fewer than twenty-seven different ways to light a campfire, some of which made use of certain enemy attributes. If nothing else, this video speaks volumes about the richness of the gameplay systems in this episode!

Clearly, even the most ordinary routines are rendered at a level of detail never before seen in a *Zelda* game... and rarely seen elsewhere either, even in RPGs developed for PCs. In the last making of video, featuring all the main members of the development team that worked with producer Eiji Aonuma, each of the team members mentions how much they enjoyed the way food was represented in the game, which may help to explain the huge number of ingredients seen in *Breath of the Wild* and their importance to its gameplay.

Since video games are a medium that grows richer with the creations and discoveries of everyone in the industry, there's really no shame in recognizing the brilliance of a competitor's work and paying tribute to it by using its ideas in a different way. On many occasions, *Breath of the Wild* gives players the feeling that the first step its creators took in bringing their ideas to fruition was by looking at what worked well in other games and thinking about how they could use it within the logic of their own game. Just as Fumito Ueda could never have created *ICO*, *Shadow of the Colossus* or *The Last Guardian* if he hadn't been deeply inspired by *Another World* and *Prince of Persia*, *The Legend of Zelda: Breath of the Wild* surely wouldn't have been such a successful contribution to the open world genre without plenty of inspiration from earlier games.

What players seemed to appreciate most about *Breath of the Wild* was that Nintendo had managed to provide a fun, bug-free, and technically clean open world experience, after years of players giving Western developers in the genre a pass for certain technical shortcomings that were assumed to be inevitable. From their earliest interactions with the game, players voiced their surprise at the near-total lack of bugs in a game of this size. How had Nintendo managed to achieve such a high level of polish that it had eliminated many defects generally believed to be an inherent feature of all open world games, even with an in-world game the size of Kyoto? As we saw earlier, the reasons mainly have to do with an omnipresent internal testing process that asked everyone involved to contribute their time and expertise to guarantee the level of quality that Nintendo demanded. Thanks to *Breath of the Wild*, we now know that the vast scale of an open world is still compatible with a high degree of technical stability, provided that every member of the development team is working in the same direction.

A WORLD WITHOUT LIMITS

Breath of the Wild's most impressive achievement, though, is not simply the fact that it easily bears comparison to the best representatives of the open world genre, but the ways in which it opens up new possibilities for that genre. Merely by offering the ability to climb virtually any surface or object, giving every player the opportunity to explore the game freely and without constraints, the title finds a way to leave its own indelible mark on the video game landscape. Anyone who has tried this *Zelda* episode for a few hours will find themselves constantly running into the limits of their environment in other games that don't provide the same degree of freedom, whether by trying to climb where it's not allowed or by leaping from high places in hopes of unfurling the equivalent of a paraglider. Of course, Link's skills as an explorer in *Breath of the Wild* were carefully designed to push players to keep venturing beyond what they see at first glance, even if it means taking completely new paths to get there. Able to climb any surface for as long as his stamina holds out, the protagonist ends up scaling all sorts of natural and artificial structures. But while most games designed on the open world principle try to preserve a certain degree of realism—including the *Assassin's Creed* franchise, despite being known for its hero's implausibly athletic parkour moves—*Breath of the Wild* doesn't mind bending the rules of reality a bit more than other games. For example, Link doesn't seem to need any kind of handhold to reach the top of a tree or sheer cliff face. So what if his feats of climbing seem a bit superhuman at times? Clearly, Nintendo made a specific choice not to put any limits on gameplay here and opted to emphasize players' enjoyment over questions of realism.

As a result, players must learn to cleverly exploit their environment to overcome obstacles that seem impassable at first. For example, cutting down a tree with an ax is a great way to create a makeshift bridge to cross a canyon; setting tall grass on fire, stirring up beehives, rolling heavy rocks, or firing a bow at an explosive object is often enough to take out an entire group of enemies. And what could be better than taking a shortcut anytime you like by climbing some part of the environment to avoid whatever difficulties may be blocking your path? Nothing forces us to follow the specific path laid out by the developers to get from one point to another. And if we think far enough ahead to prepare our hero for the physical challenges to come—by cooking a few dishes to increase or restore his stamina, for example—there are no barriers in *Breath of the Wild* that can't be crossed. By acquiring special powers, like the ability Link gets from the Ritos Champion to summon updrafts and fly high into the air, players can even briefly extend the hero's own physical limits to test out other new approaches—perfect for getting us to try out the game in all kinds of different ways. There aren't many other titles that we can approach however we choose without running into some aspect of the original game design that spoils our fantasies of life as an all-powerful adventurer.

The result is all the more impressive in that it also brings a breath of fresh air to the series by introducing a way of playing that has little in common with earlier *Zelda* games. On this subject, producer Eiji Aonuma had explained that his main goal was to experiment with things that the *Zelda* series had never done before, notably by creating a much larger world than the ones seen in earlier installments. With the help of technological advances, it was now possible to expand the area of the in-game world to previously unheard-of dimensions, while also filling that world with secrets to keep it from feeling like an empty shell. That's why exploration is consistently rewarded in *Breath of the Wild*, even if the reward is often little more than a single treasure chest or Korok Seed. As such, the player never has to go too far before discovering a new secret—and there are so many optional objectives that it's not unusual to completely lose track of the main mission that Link was supposed to be pursuing at any given time. Even players who aren't quite so obsessed with discovering new things can engage in a bit of hunting any time they like or go searching for ingredients to cook up dishes with all kinds of useful benefits.

Another unique contribution that *Breath of the Wild* brings to the open world genre has to do with the innovative requirements involved in exploring Hyrule's harshest environments. Never before have players been asked to keep such a vigilant eye on the weather conditions and the ambient temperature, which have a direct impact on our chances of survival. It's impossible to venture more than a few yards into the snowy mountains without a warm doublet to keep us nice and cozy or to try crossing the desert without a heat-resistant outfit— let alone explore volcanic regions without some form of fire protection. And while cooked meals can provide bonuses to replace these specific outfits, their effects wear off in time, making them only a temporary alternative. So while most CRPGs are content to pack the player's inventory with various pieces of equipment that are only distinguished by this or that numerical statistic, *Breath of the Wild* adds a new layer of logic to their properties that has a direct impact on gameplay. For example, while there's nothing to stop us from combining the effects of multiple items by wearing, say, a climbing bandanna with stone armor and women's harem pants, it's only by putting on all three pieces from the same outfit that we can take advantage of the special bonus that comes with the outfit as a whole (stamina boost, increased stealth, etc.). In short, even though all this equipment isn't exactly cheap and even though certain outfits are carefully hidden in various out-of-the-way locations, wearing a perfectly matched ensemble is still the best way to survive in areas requiring increased heat resistance or immunity to fire or freezing. The rest of the time, though, players are obviously free to choose the three parts of their outfit based on their visual appearance or their armor strength—a property that can only be upgraded with help from a Great Fairy, plus a bit of cash and certain specific materials.

Mother Nature is not a tender mistress in *Breath of the Wild* and seems intent on tripping us up whenever possible, whether that means making rocks slippery when the rain starts to fall or aiming lightning bolts at anyone unfortunate enough to be caught carrying metal equipment in a storm. At night, skeletons are constantly bursting out of the ground to block our path and even the travelers we meet along the way are liable to turn against us. It's ultimately all of these things together that make this open world feel so believable, independent, and alive, even when nothing in particular is going on;

players never feel truly safe outside of a small number of villages, where only the forces of nature can disturb them.

While freely citing *Skyrim*, *The Witcher 3* and even *Grand Theft Auto* among the titles that inspired him, producer Eiji Aonuma is quick to note that *Breath of the Wild* was designed from the start with that unique *Zelda* touch in mind. The decision to base this episode in an open world environment did nothing to change the fact that the game also had to establish its identity as a part of the series—and that's precisely what led the development team to test out original gameplay elements to distinguish *Breath of the Wild* from other games in the genre. In an interview with the Japanese magazine *Famitsu*, Eiji Aonuma also hinted that the design of future *Zelda* games might again be built around the open world concept, rather than returning to a more linear structure. So it's reasonable to wonder whether the open world structure might in fact become the new norm for the series.

SAVING THE FRANCHISE WITH OPEN WORLD DESIGN?

As we have just seen, *Breath of the Wild* found the right combination of ideas to establish its place in the pantheon of titles that have been most successful in transitioning to an open world design. But it's also important to understand why the new *Zelda* game chose this path in the first place. Considering the number of franchises that had already taken the risk of trying out the open world formula (although some with more success than others), it seems obvious in hindsight that Nintendo had to take the plunge too at some point. But history has shown that this genre is not an ideal fit for every license, for two main reasons: first, the difficulty of avoiding the "empty shell" effect caused by vast yet poorly-structured worlds with no side quests truly worthy of the player's interest, and second, the risk of losing sight of a series' original spirit. On the other hand, the success that certain popular franchises had achieved by convincing their fans of the need to make the switch to an open world design, rather than staying eternally trapped within the straitjacket of an unchanging formula, certainly influenced the general orientation of *Breath of the Wild*. After all, even more than many of its contemporaries, the *Zelda* series had been frequently accused of hesitating to make any serious changes to its original structure. So the time had finally come to take the leap and find out whether the open world formula, which many fans had been hoping for and demanding for quite some time, would be enough to save the franchise from the creative doldrums it had started to drift into.

THE SIREN SONG OF THE OPEN WORLD

Although the open world formula obviously can't solve every problem, most players would see it as the best way of bringing a video game series into the modern era, regardless of its genre. As startling as it may seem in some cases, there's no denying that an incredible variety of games of all types have achieved a kind of culmination or high point with their open world episodes. While the first franchises we think of here might be Western RPG series (*The Witcher 3*), Japanese RPGs (*Final Fantasy XV, Xenoblade Chronicles X*), adventure games (*Assassin's Creed, Horizon: Zero Dawn*), action series (*GTA V*) or action-RPG games (*NieR: Automata*), it's important to remember that even games in styles that would seem to lend themselves far less easily to the open world formula have also had success with it. For example, consider the stealth series *Metal Gear Solid*, completely redesigned for its fifth episode (both in the prologue, *Ground Zeroes*, and to a greater extent in *Phantom Pain*); the racing game *Forza Horizon*, which few people would have expected to venture into this style; the puzzle game *The Witness*; and the extreme sports game *Steep*, the *Far Cry* series of FPS games, or the multiplayer co-op title *Ghost Recon Wildlands* (all three of these published by Ubisoft, which has made open world games its specialty).

This diversity shows that open world games are not a genre unto themselves, but rather a particular approach to video games or a specific mechanism that aims to broaden the gameplay possibilities in any given category of games. In addition, players' reactions have shown that as long as the developers don't completely botch the transition, fans are more interested in the wide variety of activities offered by open world games than they are in more rigidly structured games. This preference is even stronger among players who grew up with titles that were designed with more of a sandbox perspective from the beginning—including the ultimate sandbox game, *Minecraft*, as well as the reliable *Elder Scrolls* series and its *Morrowind, Oblivion*, and *Skyrim* episodes. Even in games with a more restricted scope (known as semi-open worlds), the fact that players are free to choose their objectives and leave the main quest aside to focus on optional missions undeniably adds to the fun.

A DREAM COME TRUE FOR FANS

For far too long, video games insisted on forcing non-stop guidance on players, taking them by the hand to lead them wherever they needed to go for the main quest and leaving them no opportunity to diverge from the predetermined story. Even the side quests often encountered in Western and Japanese RPGs fall far short of the idea of simply letting players loose in a vast environment to do whatever they want in whatever order they choose. From this perspective, the open world structure represents a kind of high point of game design that any series hoping to renew its formula, even just a bit, is practically required to consider sooner or later. And because this change is also a dream come true for all the fans of a given series who have dreamed of seeing it evolve beyond its usual self-imposed boundaries, we can more easily understand why many developers see the switch to an open world as almost inevitable. Unfortunately, the difficulty of this process too often leads to compromises that undermine what should be the most fundamental aspects of an open world game. For example, while *Final Fantasy XV* is certainly set in an open world, it is also a restricted world that never leaves players completely free to do whatever they want. Even something as simple as being able to drive a vehicle off-road, outside of the predefined routes, required users to add an all-terrain update that was not made available until June 26, 2017—seven months after the game first came out! In other words, there are definitely some open world games that simply lead us by the hand or even actively restrict our freedom of exploration, whether by preventing us from going to certain locations at certain times or by blocking our progress with impassible invisible walls. What players really care about, then, is not so much the ability to explore a huge world without loading screens, but the ability to do as they please with no constraints. This is precisely what so-called "sandbox" games are all about: giving us the tools we need so that we can draw on the available gameplay mechanics to achieve whatever goals we set for ourselves. It seems clear that if *Breath of the Wild* had simply allowed us to go anywhere we wanted, but without giving us the ability to use the environment and everything in it to let our imaginations run wild, it would not have been such a success.

Still, reimagining the world of Hyrule for the open world formula was bound to bring radical change to a franchise as rigidly structured as *Zelda* can sometimes be, making it difficult to see how Nintendo would manage any kind of smooth or gentle transition to the new design. So the announcement of an open world installment, with all the risky changes it implied, hit the gaming press like a bomb. Among other things, the franchise is full of well-established elements that seem to go directly against the very idea of an open world. For example, other than the first episode, no *Zelda* game allows the player to enter a dungeon without first acquiring some specific object to prove that the order of events laid out by the developers has been respected. In other words, the very essence of the series lies in acquiring certain key objects at specific moments— and as a result, the adventure unfolds "on rails," according to a predefined sequence. Another constant in the franchise is the way in which every puzzle is carefully designed to be solved with one particular weapon. One switch will only react to an action relating to the crossbow, for example, while another requires that Link use a bow and arrow, and a third can only be triggered by the hookshot. While this description is obviously very abstract, any *Zelda* fan can attest to the strictly codified nature of the various puzzles in the series, most of which can only be solved in a single specific way. With an awareness of how aspects like these and many others like them have defined the franchise over the years, we can better understand how risky the transition to an open world design might seem for a series like *The Legend of Zelda*.

In leaving aside the classic pattern in which the hero alternates between village visits and dungeon exploration with little more than a brief glance at the surrounding environment, *Breath of the Wild* invites players to consider another way of experiencing the series. With this new approach, the focus is no longer on methodically making our way through one dungeon after another to solve puzzles and accumulate items and keys, but on taking the time to appreciate the world around us, observing the beauty of nature, and experiencing the pure amazement of long voyages that redefine our understanding of how vast a video game world can feel.

And yet, the imposing size of *Breath of the Wild*'s world does not make it any less enjoyable to explore. As we have already seen, the large number of secrets to be found and their strategic placement on the world map consistently reward the most meticulous exploration.

In the end, the game's designers seem to have found an ideal middle ground between an overly compartmentalized and hyperactive world, and one that is too vast and empty to hold our interest. Players are neither frustrated by an environment that's too small nor discouraged by its immensity. And while there is a tendency with open world games in general to fetishize the size of the world, as if a bigger world always meant a better game, this *Zelda* episode, as well as certain other titles before it like *GTA IV* and *The Witcher 3*, seem to show that there may be a limit that a game should not exceed if it wants to maintain an optimal level of enjoyment. It's mainly a question of balance.

PACING AND NARRATIVE:
THE KEYS TO A SUCCESSFUL OPEN WORLD

The design approach taken in this new *Zelda* game inherently encourages players to simply explore the world and to enjoy making their way through it without any particular goal in mind. *Breath of the Wild* clearly makes every effort to make us forget the main quest and turn away from it as often as possible. We learn to spend time hunting for game, trying to tame wild animals, or just wandering around to admire or collect local plants—not to mention the countless side quests that we can choose to complete and the secrets we're constantly tempted to seek out.

In *Breath of the Wild*, we find ourselves discovering the kingdom of Hyrule in a completely different way than in earlier episodes, since we pursue the main quest not by moving the story forward, but by turning away from it to collect the hero's hidden memories and remedy his amnesia. It's not surprising, then, that the challenging process of searching for these memories turns out to be the most complex and uncertain quest in the game, since the player's only clues to their location are a handful of old photos. And of course, because these photos are over a century old, they are not always very representative of the environments in today's world, deeply transformed through its domination by the Calamity. So if we want to have any reasonable chance of finding all of these hidden memories, the only option is to meticulously explore the most distant corners of Hyrule and forget any thought of going from one memory to the next in a straight line.

If additional proof were needed that helping Link to recover his lost memory by collecting these fleeting visions of the past is the real main quest in *Breath of the Wild*, note that it's only by gathering all of these memories that players can unlock the real ending sequence after defeating the Calamity—a brief conversation between Link and Zelda that starts after the main closing cinematic is finished. Ultimately, how many side missions we complete or how many Shrines we discover is less important than it is to learn, at the same time as the main character, what happened one hundred years ago—and who the people are who made Link into the hero we see in the game.

On this point, *Breath of the Wild* achieves remarkable success where so many games before it had stumbled. In most games, the freedom conferred by the open world comes at the detriment of the narrative, with the vast number of optional activities leading us to gradually lose track of the main storyline, especially when players feel obliged to complete them solely to power up their character's abilities. By spreading themselves too thin, many games thus make the mistake of losing the player in a jumble of uninteresting objectives that are not sufficiently in tune with the main story to ensure a convincing narrative experience.

If we were forced to give an opinion on whether *Breath of the Wild* succeeds in resolving the real difficulty with open worlds—that is, whether it manages to create a fully believable world, even to the point of regularly distracting us from the main quest when we are technically supposed to be saving Hyrule— then the answer would be an unqualified yes. Spending time on activities not directly linked to our primary mission does nothing to undermine the cohesion of the world in which the game is set. And diverging from the main storyline never makes us want to give up on the adventure; on the contrary, it strengthens our desire to come back to it each time we resolve one of the many mysteries surrounding us. So what really makes *Breath of the Wild*'s open world a success is that it makes us feel that everything we do within it is part of a coherent experience.

Rushing right through the adventure in a straight line, by focusing solely on the Divine Beasts or going to challenge Ganon immediately at Hyrule Castle, is only an option after we've already finished the game at least once, unless we want to miss out on its core essence. Of course, one might respond that this is true of most open world games, but we have to give *Zelda* credit for pushing this idea even further, if only because developing Link's most basic physical abilities (hearts and stamina) requires that we at least head out to find some of the one hundred and twenty Shrines hidden throughout the world.

Even more importantly, *Breath of the Wild* avoids the pitfalls of a poorly-paced open world filled with repetitive and uninspiring quests that bore players to death and leave them with just one desperate wish: to get back to the main storyline as quickly as possible. Here, even though the rewards are almost always fairly meager, the desire to complete each side mission comes from our reluctance to miss out on some new find that could make our experience of the game that much richer. Players who were disappointed with the long, drawn-out side missions in *Final Fantasy XV* and their tendency to leave us feeling like we were missing the most important aspects of the story by getting distracted from the urgency of the situation, may be surprised by the way in which this *Zelda* game justifies the need to get off the beaten path. In *Breath of the Wild*, the choice to present the narrative through memories helps to reduce the sense of urgency of Link's mission as the chosen one. Wandering aimlessly around the world doesn't conflict with the main storyline, since it is actually the only logical way to maximize our ability to take down the monster who has already been wreaking havoc on Hyrule for a full century. Players never feel guilty for taking advantage of the wide-ranging freedom offered by the open world, even if it means putting off the inevitable moment when they will have to face Ganon and bring their adventure to a close. The time needed for a player to discover all the main secrets of the kingdom of Hyrule on their own can be estimated at some 150 hours, and considerably more for a "completionist" run in which the player locates all nine hundred Korok Seeds and fills in the whole Compendium. The most amazing thing is that the time we spend with this game never seems excessive and that none of its many side offerings ever feel superfluous or trivial enough to simply skip over.

It's also interesting to note that the approach taken by *Breath of the Wild* doesn't require players to start a second "New Game+" to gain access to all the game's secrets. In fact, once our main foe has been defeated, the autosave feature sends us back to just before the final battle, and we don't receive any special bonus. The player's recent victory doesn't seem to have had any impact on the world. Instead, we are simply encouraged to discover as many secrets as we can before the point of no return—proof yet again that the so-called main quest is actually one of the least important objectives in the adventure or, in any case, the least urgent.

Ultimately, even though an excess of freedom isn't necessarily the key to transforming a series that's unprepared for the transition to an open world design, the example of *Breath of the Wild* shows that when used wisely, that kind of freedom can bring an old franchise to lofty new heights. And in the end, it's better to take the risks that come with completely reshaping the image of a series so that an open world approach makes sense than to keep clinging to symbolic aspects at any cost, even after they've outlived their usefulness.

MASTERING THE MAP OF AN IMAGINARY WORLD

THE HERITAGE OF *DARK SOULS*

Surprised by *Breath of the Wild*'s new orientation and how unusually demanding it was in terms of the skill required of players, fans were quick to compare it to the *Souls* games (*Demon's Souls*, *Dark Souls 1* through *3*, and *Bloodborne*) produced by FromSoftware. But in fact, although the early stages of the game are enough to scare off anyone who was expecting gameplay as permissive as in older *Zelda* games, it soon becomes clear that the gameplay systems in *Breath of the Wild* offer enough subtle hints and solutions to help us bypass the toughest fights and other obstacles to our progress in the game, if only through clever use of the bonuses provided by cooked dishes.

Even so, the comparison with the *Souls* series is not so far off the mark. Although the gameplay in the Nintendo game bears little similarity to that of the famous FromSoftware titles, we can still identify certain commonalities. For example, unless we limit ourselves to just the few quests that are indispensable to completing the game in a straight line, the only way to truly master the world we discover in *Breath of the Wild* is by developing a mental map of it. This decision to put the concept of spatial location and structure on a pedestal is the greatest heritage of *Dark Souls* (unless it is simply a coincidental convergence of game design). Walking through this new kingdom of Hyrule, even for just a few hours, is enough to give us a subconscious feel for its geography, allowing us to find our way through the game's different regions more by taking mental pictures of its environments than by constantly referring to the map.

This is only possible because the creators of this world took care to give each location a completely distinct character—especially in the villages, each of which has its own unique style, but also in more out-of-the-way regions where we can easily find any number of unique landmarks without even having to look for them. Through its ruined architecture or simply the subtle outlines of mountain ranges that often extend as far as the eye can see, Hyrule's geography is filled with enough subconscious reference points for us to orient ourselves without difficulty.

FUMITO UEDA'S LEGACY

This feature of the game's world also recalls the approach taken in the works of Fumito Ueda (*ICO*, *Shadow of the Colossus*, *The Last Guardian*), each of which depicts an emotionally rich journey in which players intuitively know where they are located in space relative to the places they have already explored. In *ICO*, even more than in the other two games cited here, the architecture of the fortress in which the boy and girl are held prisoner sears itself into our memory every time the camera reveals a new perspective on it.

In *Breath of the Wild*, the most obvious landmark is the menacing silhouette of Hyrule Castle, now home to the Calamity, located at the center of the world map with all the other regions of the kingdom laid out around it. In fact, wherever we may find ourselves in the course of our journey, it's almost always possible to find our bearings by looking for the billowing darkness that swirls around the enormous structure. In this way, this symbolic location serves as a permanent reference point that helps to anchor the world's geography all the more firmly in our minds.

LEARNING TO SEE AGAIN

Players gradually become familiar with the world of *Breath of the Wild* by experiencing it firsthand and absorbing it into their visual memory, eventually only needing to open the map when they want to add more precise markers to help them return later to secrets that are currently inaccessible. The game continuously invites us to explore every aspect of our environment, not only for the pure pleasure of discovering what secrets it holds, but above all, to burn it indelibly into our memory. It's this intimate familiarity that allows us to recognize the places shown in the photographs for the captured memories, but also to guess which parts of the world might hold items that are missing from our collection. For in addition to all the different available quests, the game also includes a long-term task that requires the player to complete a huge "compendium" by capturing every type of object in the game on film. In other words, not only must we remember to take a picture of every enemy we encounter along the way, but we also have to take the time to find every form of plant and animal life in the new kingdom of Hyrule—not to mention every melee weapon, bow and shield in the game! The sheer size of this task is obviously far beyond that of any other mission we are asked to complete in the game, except for the hunt for the nine hundred Korok Seeds mentioned earlier. Long-time *Zelda* fans will obviously be reminded of the search for Nintendo Gallery figurines in *The Wind Waker*, which was also based on taking photographs of all the key elements of the game, including enemies and bosses—although the vast scale of *Breath of the Wild*'s world clearly takes this idea to a whole new level.

Each in their own way, a number of other titles that emphasize exploration have found ways to include a camera as a way to extend the adventure by turning it into something resembling a sightseeing vacation. One of the clearest examples of this is the photography quest added to the 3DS remake of *Dragon Quest VIII*, in which a number of different challenges and rewards were tied to taking specific snapshots that taught players to observe their environment more carefully. Quests like these are a reminder that with our finely-honed gamers' instincts, we too often forget to even look at the landscapes around us. Video games have taught us to charge straight ahead to the finish line as quickly as possible, focusing solely on the most essential elements—almost as if we were wearing blinders. In response, *Breath of the Wild* clearly aligns itself with other titles that attempt to give virtual travelers like ourselves a chance to explore a new world in the role of patient tourists, whose main goal is to get to know that world and make it our own.

MAPPING IMAGINARY WORLDS TO MAKE THEM MORE TANGIBLE?

For literature fans, this approach clearly has a lot in common with many series of novels, both older and more recent, in which the inclusion of a detailed atlas is an integral part of the reading experience. From imaginary worlds mapped with expert precision by J. R. R. Tolkien (*Lord of the Rings*, *The Hobbit*, *The Silmarillion*) to the medieval worlds created by American novelist Robin Hobb (author of the *Farseer* and *Liveship Traders* trilogies and considered as one of the leading lights of modern fantasy), the process is ultimately the same: the narrative journey of a group of travelers is presented in parallel with its visual depiction as a hand-drawn map, which becomes an inseparable aspect of the text. In each of these cases, a literary voyage through imaginary lands is grounded in the concrete imagery of the map, allowing readers to follow along with the protagonists' travels. The same applies to the adventures that make up a tabletop role-playing game, which would be nothing without the meticulous support of a gamemaster who takes care to ensure that the players' characters progress through the game world in a way that's consistent with the carefully-designed map.

While an in-game map is almost always considered an indispensable part of any video game, it's all too easy in most cases to simply feel one's way along blindly, on autopilot, through a virtual world that's bursting with map markers. But *Breath of the Wild* actually makes exploration easier by encouraging players to orient themselves to real landmarks in the world, simply by recognizing the places they've already explored. In addition, the fact that the world is filled with imposing mountains implicitly urges players to climb them and get a top-down perspective on the landscape, making it easier to understand and memorize Hyrule's geography.

And if verticality is so heavily emphasized in *Breath of the Wild*, it's because it provides the only real way of orienting oneself in the world of the game. Wherever the player looks, they know they'll be able to get there one way or another. So it's up to them to choose when and how they'll make the trip: on foot, on horseback, or by air, after hurling themselves from the top of a mountain to soar as far as possible with their paraglider.

Truth be told, if the game's territory was not so vast, we would probably be able to find our way around the different regions of Hyrule fairly easily with no need for the world map, once our senses of direction and observation were sufficiently developed. But it's clear that the map sections revealed for each region when we activate a tower are also meant to encourage us to go and find out what hides behind the many odd-sounding location names, which often recall people and locations that will be familiar to longtime fans of the series: Ruto Lake (a reference to the Zora princess from *Ocarina of Time*), Tingel Island (inspired by Tingle, the famous "fairy" who first appeared in *Majora's Mask*), Mount Daphnes (a nod to King Daphnes Nohansen Hyrule from *The Wind Waker*), and so on. The rest of the time, it's the unique topography itself that draws us in to get a closer look at strange structures like an immense labyrinth (most likely a reference to the Maze Palace in *Zelda II: The Adventure of Link*) or an unnatural-looking spiral-shaped peninsula that recalls the Spiral Jetty, an artificial structure located on the shores of Utah's Great Salt Lake.

By constantly engaging us in this way, the environment of *Breath of the Wild* makes exploration irresistible, turning the player into a modern-day Marco Polo or David Livingstone in virtual *terra incognita*.

A RESTORATIVE REVOLUTION

Rather than attempting to change the franchise step-by-step or through careful compromises, Nintendo apparently decided with *Breath of the Wild* that it would knock the dust off the *Zelda* franchise all at once by shaking up all of its established conventions. While it would have been much less risky for the company to switch over to the open world formula slowly and gradually, Nintendo made the opposite choice by wiping the slate clean and throwing out everything that might have made us nostalgic for earlier episodes. Even the main character has been stripped of his most iconic attributes, right down to the green tunic and the famous pointed cap that he had been wearing since the start of the series. But let's not get confused: the point is not so much to modernize Link's look as it is to inform players by way of this new design that they will be able to go places the series has never been before in terms of gameplay. The overall message is that only by abandoning even its most iconic elements will the franchise be able to break free of its own self-imposed constraints.

Inevitably, saying goodbye to all of these elements that have been dear to *Zelda* fans' hearts will come with its share of painful and legitimate regrets—but would we really be able to turn the page without accepting a few sacrifices? Those who are most attached to the old days can even console themselves in a roundabout way by unlocking all the green tunics from earlier episodes of the series with the amiibos for the different versions of Link (which also changes his haircut) or by completing all one hundred and twenty hidden Shrines in order to receive the "Tunic of the Wild" as a reward. Nintendo included these outfits as a kind of backdoor cameo for earlier Links, aware of fans' sometimes excessive attachment to the saga's most venerable symbols. But at the risk of irritating certain hardcore fans, artistic director Satoru Takizawa told *Polygon* in an interview dated March 10, 2017, that he didn't consider the young Hylian's clothes as iconic as his pointy ears. More precisely, he explained that as high-resolution graphics have become more realistic, it has become more difficult to make Link's cap look "cool," as he put it. To illustrate his point, he mentioned the exaggerated size of the cap that appeared in *Twilight Princess*, mocked by certain players who asked what he was hiding inside it or compared it to a windsock. But the best example is the Master Sword, the legendary blade and a genuine symbol of the series that even appears in the game's logo—and yet, in *Breath of the Wild*, acquiring this weapon is a completely optional side quest! As one of the countless mysteries that we hear about from various NPCs to fill in the blanks about past events, even the existence of the hero's sword is uncertainand only if Link manages to find his way through the endless labyrinth of the Lost Woods can he attempt to extract it from its pedestal. Although the legendary sword is not strictly necessary for Link to triumph over Ganon, it is still indestructible and provides a useful damage bonus against the gruesome creatures that occupy Hyrule Castle. The sword can even fire energy beams if our health meter is full, just like the Master Sword in the earliest episodes in the series! Not only is it optional to acquire the legendary sword, but we can also finish the adventure without ever picking up the famous Hylian Shield with its unparalleled defensive capability, leaving it to continue collecting dust in the castle's darkest dungeons.

In other words, for the creators of *Breath of the Wild*, getting rid of certain visual symbols that were previously tied to the series' identity but now seem obsolete doesn't prevent the game from reaffirming its place as a part of the franchise. Just as the saga itself has evolved over the course of its many episodes, its hero's appearance has also evolved with changing fashions and fans' changing tastes—none of which has compromised the vision that players have formed of him in the years since the first *Zelda* game was released.

CLOSING THE DOOR ON OLD-SCHOOL DUNGEONS

Along the same lines, one of *Breath of the Wild*'s most radical breaks with its predecessors has to do with how it handles everything that relates to the design of the saga's iconic dungeons. Whereas these temples were once vast and sprawling affairs, spread out over multiple floors and rooms that each held its share of puzzles and battles, the new game completely reconsiders the way in which players explore them, due to a fundamental change in their very nature. The dungeons are no longer just hostile locations that players pass through on a linear path—they are Divine Beasts and thus semi-living creatures in their own right, integrated into the environment and the story and operated by control terminals with very specific effects. The redesign is so audacious and innovative that it quickly makes up for any bad feelings over the lack of challenging enemies other than the boss and the absence of the usual key that players can only get their hands on after an exhausting search. In the new dungeons, there is no longer any need for the old-fashioned organization into multiple rooms that players have to make their way through one at a time; indeed, what makes the dungeons in *Breath of the Wild* so unique is that they form a unified whole in which no one element stands alone. At their core, they are machines designed in a logical and functional way to look and move like animals, towering over the player from an imposing height. In addition, the terminals' innovative design allows us to rotate a given environment, flip it over, or make other unexpected changes, so that our path through each such "dungeon" feels completely unpredictable. For example, with the Divine Beast Vah Ruta, which resembles a giant elephant, the player must raise the creature's trunk to a specific height to put out a fire with the stream of water that's constantly flowing out of it, then lower it to climb up the trunk, which is essentially just a movable wall of the dungeon. On the wings of the Divine Beast Vah Medoh, which looks like a gigantic bird, interacting with the dungeon map lets us tilt the wings more or less steeply on one side in order to facilitate access to far-off places perched at dizzying heights. On Vah Naboris, the camel-like dungeon in the Gerudo desert, we have to separately turn three rings located at the beast's head, in the middle of its body, and near its tail, changing the dungeon interior so that Link can make his way through it. Finally, for the salamander Vah Rudania that is climbing the side of the Gorons' volcano, we have to rotate the beast's entire body in order to get past the dungeon's many obstacles. In other words, we now have to count on our own creativity to find the winding path that leads us to each of the control terminals hidden within each Divine Beast.

In hindsight, it's safe to say that this new way of exploring dungeons in *Breath of the Wild* is bold and inventive enough to overcome certain weaknesses that go along with it. While we certainly spend far less time here than in the dungeons from earlier games, and while the systematic hunt for terminals requires us to set aside our usual reflexes as players, exploring these strange places with their surrealist layouts is no less impressive an experience. Forced to combine a thoughtful approach based on pure observation with careful analysis of the map, which has to be rotated all around to reveal all of its secrets, players now end up viewing each dungeon as a single integrated puzzle to be solved. The feeling of victory is all the greater knowing that our survival ultimately depended on our ability to make clever use of each Divine Beast's unique controls, with the slightest false step being immediately punished by a fall from great heights—or simply by finding ourselves unable to make any further progress.

In light of the game's extraordinary size, we can easily find ourselves wondering whether *Breath of the Wild* couldn't have squeezed in at least one more dungeon of this type before Link enters Hyrule Castle for the final confrontation, but not all players would consider this to be a genuine flaw. Upon further reflection, it's true that keeping the classic formula of castles laid out as a collection of individual rooms, each bursting with enemies, would have been incompatible with the overall orientation of this new *Zelda* game. Even so, this could be an interesting point to improve upon for the future of the series, since many players would be curious to see how a "classic" dungeon (but longer and more complex) could be effectively integrated into an open world structure. Meanwhile, the decision to turn away from individual puzzles is less controversial than it might be, since there are plenty of puzzles in the one hundred and twenty optional Shrines scattered throughout the world. The game also adds an important innovation with the Shrines by making puzzle-solving an integral part of mini-dungeons that are designed to develop our logical sense and our ability to find creative solutions. Even locating the Shrines in the first place is a challenge in itself, since they can only be discovered by thoroughly exploring the vast world of the game or by completing certain very specific quests. In one case, for instance, we have to interpret the verses of an ancient legend to guess the time of day at which we can make a certain Shrine appear by firing an arrow toward the sun—giving a general idea of the type of challenge that the game confronts us with here. As a concrete embodiment of the challenges proposed by the ancient mummy-like descendants of the Sheikah, each of these Shrines provides an opportunity to better grasp the subtleties of this episode's new gameplay systems. Whether the solution to a given Shrine relies on clever use of different rune powers (bombs, ice pillars, magnetism, stasis) or on perfect mastery of our movements, their long-term effect is to improve our chances of beating the game by helping us to improve our skills at the same time as the hero. Rewarded with Spirit Orbs, symbols of courage that can boost his health or stamina meters (four Orbs can be traded for one additional heart or one unit of stamina), Link becomes stronger while the player who controls him acquires a new set of survival instincts. Finishing the Shrine challenges never feels like an obligation, but it is the most pragmatic way to enjoy the game by combining useful training with entertaining gameplay. It's also worth noting that each Shrine we discover immediately becomes available as a teleportation point, making it considerably easier to make our way around Hyrule.

Interestingly, all of the rune powers are unlocked right at the start of the game as we complete the handful of shrines on the Great Plateau—presumably in order to help us get rid of certain automatic reflexes that have no place in this new world. This starting area therefore serves as a kind of tutorial, but oriented more toward breaking our old habits as longtime *Zelda* fans than teaching us to deal with the challenges to come. By extension, these first four Shrines on the Great Plateau can be seen as a nod to the initial stage that generally precedes our discovery of the main quest in earlier *Zelda* episodes, like the search for the three medallions in *A Link to the Past* or the three Spiritual Stones in *Ocarina of Time*. As such, players can't help wondering about the true nature of these Shrines, since they don't yet know whether these are the game's "real" dungeons or how they might evolve over the course of the adventure. The challenges offered in this introductory stage are so brief and so simple that experienced players may start to feel a bit concerned, especially when faced with a world map that seems intentionally designed to make us think that the open world is no larger than this initial region. Only after playing for a few hours do we realize how dizzyingly vast the outlines of this world really are, with an astronomical number of secrets to discover and no less than one hundred and twenty optional Shrines hidden throughout the game. But by then, the player has had sufficient "training" to start looking for them in earnest.

The other aspect that makes the shrines in *Breath of the Wild* such an impressive *tour de force* is that, despite the mind-boggling number of them we are asked to explore, each one feels incredibly creative and fresh. We never have the feeling that we're seeing the same puzzle for the umpteenth time; instead, skill and careful planning alternate with occasional moments of extreme precision, like when we have to use the controller's gyroscope function to complete games of skill reminiscent of the old *Super Monkey Ball* series. Whether we're asked to use our rune powers to get past an obstacle, keep a cool head as we follow a path filled with pitfalls, or carefully manipulate the controller to guide a ball rolling over an unstable platform, each of these trials resonates in its own unique way for every player. In effect, they cover all the different situations we would have expected to find in the game's main dungeons—but in an "à la carte" mode that lets us pick and choose our puzzles as we play through Shrines around the edges of the main adventure.

Unlocked using the Sheikah Slate that Link picks up at the start of the adventure, these mysterious Shrines bear a certain resemblance to the hidden tombs in the *Assassin's Creed* series. Their primary function is to test our ability to master all of the Slate's many features, which include letting Link use a magnetic field to move different objects around, throw round and square remote bombs, raise ice pillars from any body of water, or temporarily stop the flow of time—not to mention the detector function that highlights nearby objectives with its built-in camera. Adding to the diversity of the Sheikah Slate's secrets, many Shrines require players to switch among these different powers to overcome an increasingly complex range of puzzles. These puzzles also highlight the game's inherent generosity in that each Shrine can be completed in a number of different ways, depending on each player's creative ideas and discoveries. Given all this, it's hard not to see the shrines as an evolution from the dungeons from earlier episodes in the series, even if their somewhat sanitized and repetitive environments put them a bit out of sync with the rest of the game and its emphasis on nature in all its wildest forms.

Toward a new set of gameplay routines

Two distinct attempts to unsettle series diehards quickly come to light when we first dive into *Breath of the Wild*. At the start of the game, as we have just seen, the focus is on leaving aside the basic elements that were once so essential to the series; but as the game progresses, players are also faced with an unexpected influx of new gameplay mechanics that would have been unimaginable in earlier episodes. The result is a complete redefinition of the overall gameplay, through the addition of new rules that might not have seemed relevant to the well-established model that the series had built for itself over the years.

While unlimited exploration of the newly open world through the ability to climb is certainly one feature of *Breath of the Wild* that serves to redefine the way we play, it's far from being the only one. Another aspect of this transformation is the addition of all kinds of new constraints. Whether they relate to Link's physical attributes (his limited stamina and the need to eat food to survive) or to the ever-changing weather conditions (learning to avoid lightning and wear the right sort of clothes for each region), these constraints force us to reconsider our priorities as experienced players. Since the environment is no longer filled with little hearts hidden in the grass or generously dropped by defeated enemies, players learn to keep up their energy by cooking, which in turn requires learning to hunt and build a fire with whatever resources come to hand.

Before long, players acquire the same survival instincts as any other adventurer who finds themselves thrown into an unplanned expedition with no end in sight. Because we don't know how long our journey will last, nor what might be lying in wait behind the next hilltop, we learn to tread carefully where once we charged boldly through the landscapes of earlier *Zelda* games. Even the simple fact that Link now has physical abilities rarely seen elsewhere in the series, like jumping and climbing, makes us aware of the increased responsibility we bear. Players are no longer led by the hand, but totally free to move and act however they please in an adventure that is completely their own from start to finish.

Skyward Sword as idea incubator

And yet, even as these new elements radically define the very nature of the franchise, they didn't appear out of thin air quite as suddenly as one might think. In fact, there was another episode that laid the groundwork for this installment a few years earlier, and that tried in its own way to explore some of the new ideas laid out in *Breath of the Wild*. That episode, of course, was *Skyward Sword*. Released for the Wii console in November 2011, *Skyward Sword* had already taken the bold step of introducing a stamina limit on the movements and actions the hero could take, along with the idea of durability for shields and the ability to upgrade certain key items. The game also took place in a world with a more fragmented structure and even introduced the notion of the Sailcloth, a makeshift parachute that Link could use to slow his fall. Of course, since most of the game's action took place high in the sky, Link had to fly from one floating island to the next in *Skyward Sword*. And although the Sailcloth was not intended to let Link fly freely wherever he chose, but simply to get him to the ground in one piece, it was still quite obviously the spiritual predecessor to the paraglider.

Weapon durability was also first introduced in *Skyward Sword*, and its treatment in *Breath of the Wild* was again a logical extension of the original idea. The earliest trailers for the new *Zelda* game had already highlighted Nintendo's clear desire to move away from the series' most rigidly established routines and adopt most of the typical mechanics of Western RPGs. One sign of this shift is the huge variety of available items, including a vast selection of weapons and equipment with numerical statistics. In *Breath of the Wild*, players now have to keep an eye on their weapons' durability to avoid having them break. This design decision is a perfect illustration of the enormous risk Nintendo was taking by going back to square one with some of the saga's most iconic gameplay routines and adopting a new approach that seemed light-years away from the days when Link's inventory included only a handful of key items that were the same in every episode! Of course, the decision to offer players such a fragile arsenal of weapons would not have been nearly as interesting if they could simply repair them whenever they liked. Setting aside the special case of Octoroks—monsters that can turn rusted weapons into cleaner, more powerful ones by swallowing them and spitting them back out—*Breath of the Wild* generally requires us to accept the idea that all of our weapons and shields are disposable and replaceable (except, of course, for the Master Sword, although even that mighty blade may only be used in limited ways). On the other hand, the game encourages us to deliberately attack our enemies with worn-out weapons to take advantage of the extra damage they do on their last hit before breaking, which certainly makes it easier to say goodbye. As cruel as it can be to lose a high-quality blade in this way, we can console ourselves with the thought that the resulting victory will let us pick up any weapons dropped by our defeated enemies, not to mention the many other opportunities to grab all kinds of weapons that no one else seems interested in claiming. In short, by going even further with the concept of weapon durability, the creators of *Breath of the Wild* turned what had been merely an added constraint in *Skyward Sword* into an exciting new aspect of the gameplay. We can also see *Skyward Sword*'s legacy in the artistic direction of *Breath of the Wild*, which takes on a similar tone through its use of cel shading (a technique that produces a cartoon-like visual effect), but applied to more realistic character models than the ones used in *The Wind Waker*. Though distinct, the artistic styles of *Skyward Sword* and *Breath of the Wild* still have a number of clear similarities that help both games to avoid either an overly childish look or an excess of realism.

With each new addition to the series, *Zelda* attempted to refresh the formula, with varying degrees of success, by introducing new ideas to break free of the boundaries that the franchise had set for itself. These included the parallel worlds in *A Link to the Past*, the untamable ocean in *The Wind Waker*, Link's ability to transform into a wolf in *Twilight Princess*, or the touch controls on the DS episodes. And more than any other installment, *Skyward Sword* deserves to be considered as an incubator of innovation that ultimately gave rise to most of the boldest new elements in *Breath of the Wild*. But it's the new *Zelda*'s willingness to take big risks that most clearly explains its undeniable success in finally achieving the renewal that the franchise creators had been seeking for years. As if making bold change wasn't enough—and only the boldest possible change would do.

FREEDOM TO BE CREATIVE

MULTIPLE DEGREES OF FREEDOM

Even the title *Breath of the Wild* holds out a tantalizing promise of a journey in which nothing is forbidden and everything is permitted. Clearly, the choice of the word "wild" has less to do with a savage and hostile world than the idea of a natural environment left to thrive on its own, in part because the reference to the "breath" of wild nature evokes pleasant surprises—like the animals we are able to tame, the long idyllic walks, and meetings with the other people of Hyrule—far more than any thought of danger. Of course, by the end of their long wanderings, many players will still shudder at the mere thought of their terrifying run-ins with Guardians that pursued them to their deaths or with the fearsome centaurs known as Lynels. But, like the image of Link on the cover of the European version of the game, turning to face the viewer with a dreamy look in his eye as he stands on a lush green hilltop, there's no doubt that this adventure was primarily meant as a sincere invitation to enjoy the natural world around us. And what better way to enjoy it than by taking the time to see it up close along whatever winding paths our imaginations suggest to us?

While *Breath of the Wild*'s title makes no direct reference to freedom, that concept is still clearly implied and lends its enticing aura to the game as a whole. Like the pet dog who responds to the *Call of the Wild* in Jack London's classic novel by surrendering to his irrepressible natural instincts, players give in to the siren song of *Breath of the Wild* in hopes of catching a glimpse of the kind of freedom we so rarely find in video games. There is probably no need to spend any more time here on the core elements of the game that most clearly reinforce this genuine feeling of freedom (climbing, the paraglider, the constant sense of discovery, and the ability to go wherever we like after the first few hours of the game). But there also seems to be something else hidden behind the creators' obsession with doing everything in their power to encourage that sense of freedom. Could it be that they've hit upon the most instinctive way to speak directly to players' imaginations and inspire their creativity?

Obviously, freedom takes many forms in this game, from freedom of movement (we can choose our destination and our preferred way of getting there) and narrative freedom (through the order in which we collect the memories and finish the dungeons) to freedom of action, in the sense of choosing to act according to our own logic. It is this last type of freedom that seems to be the most heavily emphasized throughout the game, because in the end, it seems that no quest, no battle, and no puzzle is really completely scripted. Designed with the goal of always offering players multiple ways to achieve any particular objective, the game consistently rewards creativity—an approach that is only possible because the game's many puzzles (situations encountered in the open world and problems to solve in the Shrines) were not created on a case-by-case basis. Instead, they are directly grounded in a physics engine that opens a much wider range of possibilities than anything the designers could have planned for and written down. Their richness and diversity therefore go far beyond the simple ability to solve this or that puzzle in multiple different ways. They are revealed over the long term in the discoveries made by players themselves, who show the whole world through their own amateur videos how anyone with enough ingenuity and creativity can push past the boundaries originally imagined by the developers. Of course, these demonstrations often require perfect mastery of the game's most demanding gameplay mechanics, but even the creators of *Breath of the Wild* might well be surprised by some of the more experimental ideas put forward by certain players.

Rare indeed are the titles that remove all constraints on our imagination by providing tools to let us break free of the rules of the game without actually telling us how to do so. In a shift that is in many ways quite similar to what has made *Minecraft* such an immensely popular game, many fans are most impressed with *Breath of the Wild* not for everything it directly offers us... but for everything it turns out to be hiding! Everything about this game seems to imply that we can test all of its limits to make even our craziest ideas a reality. We will be looking at some of these surprising discoveries later on as proof that players can easily complete the adventure without using more than a tiny percentage of the resources that the game has to offer.

But before diving into all the fascinating ways in which players can push the game to its absolute limits, we cannot conclude this brief discussion of freedom in *Breath of the Wild* without mentioning another form of narrative freedom that has to do with the completion of its countless optional side quests. Closely following the model proposed by *The Witcher 3*, the new *Zelda* game leaves it to us to untangle the profusion of scripted quests that are more or less closely related to our primary objective: defeating the Calamity. In *Breath of the Wild*, then, there is not just a single goal to accomplish, but several different main quests that are updated as we advance through the game and regularly complemented by a dizzying number of new side quests. These include seventy-six optional missions and forty-two Shrine missions, besides the fifteen quests that relate directly to the main storyline. Of course, these are completely separate from the revelations contained in the hidden memories and must also be distinguished from the many secrets found by exploring the world (the hunt for the nine hundred Korok Seeds, the buried treasures, the dragons, the materials required to get the fairies' help in upgrading our equipment, etc.). But they help to personalize our experience of the game and make each playthrough unique by leaving us entirely free to either help the local population or not.

By extension, this narrative freedom also comes in part from the enormous size of the open world. That sense of scale is also reflected in the mega-puzzles contained in the four dungeons, which are themselves moving giants to be controlled in any order we choose. As in games like *Soul Reaver*, *Shadow of the Colossus*, and *God of War*, the game draws on the immense size and uncontrollable movements of the Divine Beasts to intimidate players who initially have no idea where to start when taking them down. Especially since the order in which we choose to activate the different control terminals can make it more or less difficult to explore these organic dungeons, which turn and pivot in all directions at times, forcing Link to engage in a delicate balancing act. Through the wide variety of different approaches available to us at any given moment, *Breath of the Wild* avoids the frustration that can come with too strong an emphasis on scripted elements and instead leaves us with the sense of being completely in control of our own adventure. This is an important first for the series.

WHEN PLAYERS PUT THE GAME THROUGH ITS PACES

The systemic nature of *Breath of the Wild*'s gameplay reflects its creators' desire to give players all the tools they need to break free of the game's constraints—proof that they fully trust players to make good use of those tools. Games built on the sandbox model have frequently shown that a significant portion of the gaming public is eager to make use of such tools to explore the unexplorable and see what their favorite titles are made of. With the advent of amateur videos on the Internet, the most inventive players know they've got a good chance to generate some serious buzz if they're the first to point out an unexpected find—especially one that's not based solely on exploiting a glitch in the game that will likely be fixed in the next update. As a result, there has been a proliferation of YouTube channels since the game's release that examine the hidden possibilities of *Breath of the Wild*, whereas most games don't get much more than a few walkthrough videos that are all more or less the same. But because it relies on a realistic representation of the laws of physics and especially because it doesn't impose any limits on in-game experimentation, the Nintendo title lends itself spectacularly to these sorts of tests, whether they're done just for fun or with the specific goal of "breaking" the game experience.

The second approach includes the phenomenon known as speedrunning, in which players attempt to complete a game as quickly as possible, preferably without using any tools that are not available under normal conditions (except in the case of "tool-assisted speedruns," or TAS). A successful speedrun mainly relies on complete mastery of the gameplay mechanisms, but can also make use of any relevant bugs in the game engine. As unlikely as it may seem, players quickly figured out how to rush through the main quest in *Breath of the Wild* in under four hours—only to be outdone by other experts who could make their way straight to the fight with Ganon in less than an hour and a half! Whatever tricks are used along the way (like using an amiibo right from the start of the game to unlock the legendary horse Epona and ride through the world more quickly), these impressive feats line up with what producer Eiji Aonuma had promised when he said that players would be able to take on Ganon immediately if they felt up to the challenge. Even many months after the game's release, hardcore players continue to take part in fierce competitions every week, with or without the bonuses provided by amiibos or DLC. As of June 15, 2017, the record holder was the American speedrunner Ikkitrix, who completed the game in 39 minutes and 57 seconds from start to finish on the Wii U version—along with another run in which he completed all the shrines in just 8 hours and 31 minutes. As if to prove that the game has an immense amount of content even for speedrunners, the best time for a 100% run is 33 hours and 41 minutes, achieved by the French gamer Xalikah. Competition in this area is intense, so these records may well have been broken many times over by the time this book is published, but these examples clearly show how many strange and unusual ways there are to complete this adventure. But even though the tutorial on the Great Plateau and the final battle with Ganon are the only parts of the game that are strictly required, players still have to find some way to survive and progress effectively with just three hearts and a nearly empty inventory. And let's not forget that skipping the four main dungeons means that Link also has to defeat their fearsome guardians before the final face-off with Ganon, whose health meter is still at full strength—enough to intimidate all but the most audacious and experienced players.

The reason why the game is able to give players so much latitude in their approach is that it is filled with subtle nuances that are built right into its design. Players get the feeling that even the most ordinary objects in the game can be used in ways just waiting to be discovered—and indeed, the developers made every effort to keep that idea in mind throughout the creative process. So even though it's never made explicit, we find out through hands-on experience how different gameplay possibilities can lead to ingenious new discoveries that make the game even more fun to play. And it's precisely these countless subtle touches that are so fascinating once we start to dive a little deeper into *Breath of the Wild*. For example, the Magnesis rune, which allows Link to control metal objects found in certain locations in the world, has a hidden potential that's far from obvious at first. Beyond its main function, which consists of lifting metal plates and crates into the air to discover buried secrets or to use them as projectiles, Magnesis can also be seen as an extension of our arms. This implies that we can reach an otherwise inaccessible chest, for example, simply by lifting a metallic object and pushing it into the chest to knock it down. Discovering just one such indirect use of any given power reminds us to keep our minds open to the possibilities offered by all of the different runes, even beyond their most obvious function.

As we begin to realize just how carefully the game's different mechanics have been worked out in all their most subtle nuances, it's both amusing and strangely impressive to discover that we can change the color and the properties of Chuchu Jelly by bringing it into contact with natural elements. If we need a specific type of jelly, all we need to do is grab a bit of blue jelly (the most common kind) from our inventory and turn it into red or yellow jelly by exposing it to fire or lightning. Beyond special types of arrows, any weapon infused with one of these natural elements is enough to trigger the expected chemical change, although changing weather conditions can also interfere at any time to generate unexpected effects.

While we're on the subject of the weather, we should point out that this is yet another aspect of *Breath of the Wild* that's filled with surprises. We generally discover the subtleties of the weather system through some unfortunate accident, like the fact that we need to put away our metal equipment during storms to avoid being struck by lightning—but on the other hand, that means we can trap our enemies by intentionally throwing a metal object at their feet. Along the same lines, we might accidentally learn during our wanderings that a quick swim in cold water provides temporary resistance to flames, or that we can stay warm even on a chilly mountaintop by holding a fire weapon. Similarly, ice-cold air freezes meat almost instantly, while burning vapors will cook it just as quickly. Because the gameplay system takes a logical realistic and thus entirely intuitive approach, it's easy for anyone to grasp its possibilities and limits with just a bit of thought. If a flaming sword can keep us warm in the snow, why not equip an ice-based weapon to keep us cool in the desert heat? Realizing that all of these things work as expected, even though many of these solutions would be inconceivable in most other video games, contributes to our awareness that *Breath of the Wild* consistently takes the player seriously. When Link is near hot lava, arrows catch fire instantly, and explosive arrows literally blow up in his face before he even has time to draw his bow. But they won't work at all if it's raining—a bit like trying to light a wet firecracker...

Since money is hard to come by in *Breath of the Wild*, truly needy players may well resort to selling cooked meals or gambling, while others will take the time to master the confusing and enigmatic experience of tracking the legendary dragons and get rich in a more elegant way by collecting their scales. Meanwhile, those who prefer patience to more risky endeavors will opt for the laborious process of collecting Star Fragments, which appear as shooting stars in the night sky—and may only reach the ground someplace very far away. Everyone will find their own method, as long as it pushes them to be clever and creative and doesn't rely too much on random chance.

In combat, since monsters tend to doze off at nightfall, we can adopt a furtive approach to make off with their weapons before they have a chance to pick them up or even neutralize them silently in their sleep. Even Hinox the cyclops has to lie down once in a while, allowing Link to take advantage of this moment of weakness to sneak past him or detach his shiny necklace with a well-placed arrow to steal the weapons that it's made from. And even if things take a turn for the worse, we can sometimes find a way to turn our enemies against one another and watch them fight it out while we escape—maybe on the back of a deer or a bear. Fortune favors the bold! Elsewhere, the chicken-like Cuccos have had a legendary reputation since *A Link to the Past* for attacking us en masse if we are foolish enough to provoke them. In *Breath of the Wild*, we can take advantage of this by turning a flock of Cuccos, more terrifying than any swarm of wasps, against a group of nearby enemies. Like many other sites that specialize in video games, *Hitek.fr* took the time to catalog a few of these carefully hidden details, even recounting the reactions of various NPCs when they see Link walking around in nothing but his boxer shorts. Link even has a special animation that shows off his biceps (or rather, his lack thereof) when we leave him to stand still for a moment in this revealing outfit.

Listing all the little tricks and unexpected moments that we can find in the game is likely an impossible task—and in any case, the fun part is to discover them for ourselves, sometimes at a certain cost, without any outside source of help to point us in the right direction. But one kind of experimentation that's definitely worth reporting, even if it means spoiling a surprise or two, is the kind that borders on exploiting an in-game glitch. These feats involve so much individual ingenuity on the player's part that there's almost no choice but to share them—and it's to YouTube-worthy exploits like these that we'll now turn our attention.

In the inventive logic of *Breath of the Wild* and drawing on the heritage of *The Wind Waker*, rafts are controlled not by paddling with an oar, but by waving a Korok Leaf to blow air into their sails. At least, that's the theory. In practice, more creative players have discovered that just like with heavy rocks, it's possible to make rafts float by attaching a few Octo Balloons dropped by defeated Octoroks... From there, it's no great leap to the idea of using the raft as a flying ship—and of course, a few skilled players got to work on this idea immediately, and quickly discovered that getting exactly where you want to go in this way requires truly extraordinary patience and precision. Before long, YouTuber "BeardBear" had posted a video to his channel to show off his highly original but extremely arduous airborne journey to Hyrule Castle on a floating raft. From there, others went even further with their improvements to raft travel, speeding up their journeys over water by using a metal object controlled with the Magnesis Rune to move the raft along faster by pushing on its mast instead of wearing themselves out blowing air into the sail. In effect, these players had turned a simple raft into a motorboat! On his own YouTube channel, Mety333 shows us how it's theoretically possible to use the Magnesis Rune (again) to transport a chariot from Death Mountain to extremely distant parts of the world, where he can then use it as a flying machine to reach the four Divine Beasts. By placing a metal crate between Link and the chariot in order to lift the chariot as high into the air as possible, the player then simply has to use the Stasis Rune to freeze the crate in place at a dizzying height. Of course, the chariot has to be parked at a very specific location so that Link can then paraglide over to the Divine Beast Vah Medoh without going through the approach stage normally required by the story. In this particular case, unfortunately, the trick fails when we discover that the dungeon is intangible and inaccessible when we approach it in such a roundabout way. In another video, Mety333's attempt to go through the dragons' dimensional portal by using the flying-machine trick combined with Revali's Gale comes to a similarly unsuccessful end. Even so, these efforts prove that the tools that the developers put in players' hands have sometimes led to results far beyond anything they originally imagined!

Tricks like these, which rely heavily on the physics of in-game elements, involve gameplay quite similar to that seen in games like *Portal* and its sequel, which were widely acclaimed for their well-designed physics-based puzzles and their realistic feel. For example, YouTuber Mety333 continues with the logic of his earlier attempts and tries to reach the other Divine Beasts by using Stasis to freeze a metallic crate and turn it into a catapult. After a few violent hits, the crate unfreezes and flies into the air at such incredible speed that the player only has to deploy his paraglider at the right moment to reach a sufficient height to glide all the way to Vah Naboris. This time, it's the Beast's laser that cuts short an otherwise legendary exploit. The Vah Ruta video is even more amusing: attempting to avoid the attacks of the beast that goes after him furiously as soon as he lands on its surface, our star player even goes so far as to try surfing on his shield to protect himself as he lands. But his perseverance is in vain, as neither Vah Ruta's trunk nor its other body parts seem to be accessible directly from his starting position.

In *Breath of the Wild*, we can never be sure that some idea is truly impossible until we have tried every possible way to make it happen. For example, one player (Nassi) tried to register a Guardian as his steed by pushing it to a stable with a chest controlled by the Magnesis Rune... after cutting off the monster's legs! This effort failed as well, since it's impossible to ride a Guardian—but it showed laudable initiative and serves as a perfect illustration of the sort of crazy things that *Breath of the Wild* invites us to try by giving us such an extreme degree of freedom.

REALISM VERSUS FUN

FINDING THE PERFECT BALANCE

Now that we know how positively *Breath of the Wild* was received by critics and gamers around the world, it's useful to look back and consider the ways in which certain onlookers might have been justified in worrying about *Zelda*'s transition to an open world design. Unlike many other franchises that had succumbed to the call of the open world model at some point in their history, one disadvantage for the Nintendo saga was its deep roots in fantastic and imaginary storytelling. For many people, the *Zelda* universe's characteristic lack of realism could only hurt its efforts to move its foundations to an open world based on stricter and more demanding rules. More specifically, the decision to include new features like stamina management, weapon and shield durability, changing weather conditions, and a limited inventory that would force players to choose which items to keep, threatened to change the very face of the franchise. There was also the risk that a tougher combat system would blunt the effectiveness of a gameplay system that longtime fans had grown accustomed to over the years. After all, changing the rules of the game in any genre always runs the risk of rejection by players who are not on board with a redesign that could potentially undermine a system that they've grown deeply attached to. In *Zelda*'s case, the fantasy aspects of the kingdom of Hyrule, which straddles the boundary between fairy tales and knightly legend, would seem to make the transition to an open world more difficult to accomplish. In any case, it was the first time the question had come up for a franchise firmly founded on rules so far outside our ordinary reality. And that's why, in order to break free of the routines that the series had been relying on for decades, *Breath of the Wild* had to tear everything down and build its open world from the ground up. Since the new rules of this style were intended to establish a more realistic tone than usual, Nintendo had to knowingly risk disrupting the foundational elements that had made the series what it was.

One of the trickiest challenges that the development team faced was to find an ideal balance between the realism of an open world and the old-school fun of playing earlier installments in the series. While players were willing to make certain concessions if it meant seeing the franchise evolve, there were still certain limits to how many new rules and restrictions they'd be willing to accept. In the end, it's amazing to realize how far the designers were able to go in reimagining the game's structure without letting its new gameplay requirements get in the way of simple entertainment.

A MORE BELIEVABLE ADVENTURE

We've already seen that in terms of square mileage, the choice of an environment nearly as large as the city of Kyoto meant that the team had to come up with a few tricks to keep players interested in exploring such an enormous world. Similarly, introducing a weather system with tangible effects on the world, along with a day/night cycle with its own direct consequences for gameplay, would never have worked without long sessions of internal playtesting. Unlike many games which only introduce changing weather conditions to make the world more realistic on a visual level, *Breath of the Wild* was able to integrate this element in a way that brought added depth to its gameplay systems. Not only does the hero have to constantly adapt his outfit to the outdoor temperature in order to survive, but his physical abilities are also affected by conditions on the ground. Without the right boots, his feet will sink into the snow, slowing him down considerably; the same is true of the hot sands of Hyrule's deserts. Similarly, walls become slippery as the rain starts to fall, making it more difficult to climb mountains—but not completely impossible if we look for more accessible and closely-spaced handholds. The wind is another constant factor that contributes more than just an added layer of realism, allowing us to fly long distances and catch updrafts with our paraglider. All of these examples show that it's not enough to simply add a few realistic elements to a virtual world to make it more believable, but that it's also essential to test their effectiveness in order to be sure that increased realism doesn't come at the cost of players' enjoyment. For example, if the designers of *Breath of the Wild* hadn't left us with any backup solutions for reaching the top of a mountain during a rain shower or if we were forced to seek shelter during thunderstorms and simply wait for them to pass, the weather system would have been nothing more than a source of frustration.

So it's in this spirit that the game incorporates a number of different tricks to subtly bypass the constraints imposed by the stamina gauge. Many players have noted that even the most prestigious games often struggle to implement this device without unnecessarily complicating the simple process of moving our character from one place to the next. In *Final Fantasy XV*, for example, it's hard to imagine that a hero as powerful as Noctis would use up his stamina so quickly when running. In *Breath of the Wild*, it's Link's inability to swim underwater that might seem a bit baffling. But to return to our question of how to successfully make use of the stamina gauge—a device that the series had already experimented with in *Skyward Sword*, as we saw earlier—the issue is ultimately resolved in an indirect way, through the wide variety of options we're given to work around the constraints it imposes. If we're just a few feet from reaching the top of a sheer cliff, a cooked meal with a simple stamina bonus will be enough to get us the rest of the way there. As for longer-term solutions, we can readily exchange our Spirit Orbs for a permanent increase in our maximum stamina, call on Revali's Gale for a quick boost... or maybe just opt for a complete mountain climber's outfit instead. Finally, we should note that although stamina is required to complete most physical actions, the weight of Link's equipment has no effect on the hero's fatigue level (unlike in *Dark Souls*)—another example of Nintendo's efforts to compromise between realism and player enjoyment.

Clearly, there's no shortage of ways to bypass the various difficulties that go along with *Breath of the Wild*'s more realistic design. In a sense, we might even see this kind of flexibility as a kind of counterweight to the search for ever-greater realism. Almost as though Nintendo had intentionally stopped halfway in order to ease its fans gently into the open world model. Then again, it could be the unintentional result of the publisher's lack of experience with a design approach taken directly from Western developers. But considering how logically the challenges and solutions fit together in *Breath of the Wild*, it seems more likely that these compromises are justified by a conscious desire to find the perfect balance between realism and entertainment. Making the game excessively demanding for no reason would threaten players' enjoyment of it, which would in turn undermine their interest in exploring and experimenting with the game. This approach would sacrifice fun for the sake of realistic physics. It would build an impenetrable wall between reality and fiction, between mere travel and a magical escape. From this point of view, it seems that we can trust Nintendo to never give up on its sacred vision of video games as a source of entertainment above all else. This is probably why *Breath of the Wild* doesn't bother keeping track of how much our equipment weighs, unlike just about every other game that uses numerical statistics for weapons. To do so would have surely been the straw that broke the camel's back in terms of the all-important balance between realism and enjoyable gameplay, given that most players were already thrown off by the need to constantly say goodbye to their old weapons and find new ones. So we can probably consider the game's occasionally lax attitude toward the new rules imposed by greater realism as a kind of necessary compromise.

THE VULNERABLE WARRIOR

This aggressive realism feels even more flagrantly intrusive in the ways it seeks to redefine our habits in combat, turning systems we've known for years on their head. Since the advent of 3D graphics and the milestone event that was *Ocarina of Time*, the *Zelda* series has established certain very specific codes for its combat sequences, notably through the "lock" feature that lets the player dodge or counterattack in an intuitive way while keeping the enemy squarely in front of them. Although *Breath of the Wild* still allows us to approach battles in this way, combat feels considerably different due to the new rules imposed here. While evasive maneuvers were once very permissive, the ability to dodge sideways or backflip out of danger now requires such precise timing that we are often more likely to trip ourselves up than our enemies. The true danger lies not so much in the specific enemy we face, but in its choice of weapon, since the sheer diversity of options (swords, spears, axes, etc.) leaves us constantly readjusting our expectations about the range and speed of enemy attacks. Given this complexity, it's nice to see that a successful dodge or perfect parry with the shield is consistently rewarded with a slow-motion effect that ensures a stylish and devastating counterattack. Because it's nearly impossible to pull off these perfect techniques every time (in contrast to earlier episodes), they are highlighted with flashy cinematic tricks that encourage us to master the subtleties of the combat system rather than seeking an easy way out. Of course, failure often means losing five or six hearts at a time, but the mastery that we acquire along the way is invaluable to our long-term success.

Probably because this new approach is completely at odds with what we'd normally expect from the series, some observers were quick to compare the combat system to that of *Dark Souls*, the paradigm example of an unforgivingly difficult game that leaves players no room for error. In reality, this comparison clearly misses the mark, since *Breath of the Wild* actually gives players more than enough ways to get around any difficulty they may encounter. Among these are obviously all the types of solutions mentioned earlier, but also the simple fact of being able to save our game at any time so that we can reload it in case of a problem—not to mention the ability to escape from even the worst situations by teleporting to whatever location we choose.

The other point that radically distinguishes the two games in their approach to combat has to do with the how our choice of weapons affects the way we play. This choice has a major impact in *Dark Souls*, but only a minor one in *Zelda*. Although a heavy two-handed ax clearly lends itself to a different range of situations than a fast-moving one-handed blade, with the former serving mainly to break the enemy's defenses while the latter lets us use a shield for defense, hand-to-hand combat shows a distinct lack of diversity in *Breath of the Wild*, despite the wide range of available weapons. If we want to test out different offensive approaches, our only real option is to use different runes or interact directly with our environment. For example, we might opt for an aerial assault by targeting explosive barrels with a bow, or finding a way to stealthily disarm our enemies in advance. The fact that objects and enemies in the game obey realistic laws of physics encourages all kinds of inventive and experimental approaches. Players know that they can use their environment to get the upper hand on their opponents, even without any special high-powered attacks.

Once a fight gets underway, the type of weapon we're holding ultimately has only a limited impact on how the battle actually unfolds. Hits and charged attacks quickly wear down our stamina, and it's not unusual to find ourselves out of breath in the middle of a fight, especially against Guardian Scouts, just because we took one too many shots from the air. In addition, even though many of the monsters we meet here are familiar from earlier *Zelda* games, they are now much smarter and more aggressive. Bosses are so quick and fearsome that we can no longer defeat them simply by learning their distinctive attack patterns. And because even the lowliest Bokoblin archers can still be pretty tough when attacking in groups, the feeling of vulnerability that we experience in every altercation keeps us alert to the dangers of a frontal assault with melee weapons. Players can no longer rely solely on their acrobatic skills to anticipate enemy attacks when their range and speed is constantly changing, especially since any mistake can now bring severe consequences.

By their very design, then, battles in *Breath of the Wild* encourage us to act carefully or even run away at times—and if that means missing out on a treasure chest or two, so be it. The developers seem to have chosen to put more emphasis on establishing a sense of fear than on Link's prowess as a warrior and on his fragility and humanity more than his strength and courage. From the player's point of view, the overall feeling may not be much like that of a *Dark Souls* game nor that of an earlier *Zelda* episode, but it fits with the idea of having to fend for oneself in a threatening environment where death can rear its head at any time.

How "mature" should a Zelda game be?

In discussing the role of realism in *Breath of the Wild*, we must also address a recurring debate that had raged since *The Wind Waker* about how "mature" the tone of each new episode should be. The fierce controversy that was unleashed with the release of that episode, which was the first to adopt an unapologetically cartoon-like artistic direction, clearly had a long-term effect on fans. From then on, the announcement of a new *Zelda* episode almost inevitably restarted the debate about whether the "cartoon" or "mature" direction was more appropriate. And yet, strangely enough, the question barely came up in connection with *Breath of the Wild*, as if the issue were no longer relevant.

For most players, it's the more mature episodes that have made the most lasting contribution to the series—especially the universally-revered *Ocarina of Time* and the later episode, *Twilight Princess,* with its decidedly dark and tormented tone. Strongly inspired by the epic aura surrounding Peter Jackson's *Lord of the Rings* movie trilogy, the latter episode embodies all the "maturity" that fans had so vehemently demanded. Shigeru Miyamoto received a standing ovation at E3 2004 when the first trailer for this game was revealed, and it was surely the melancholy and realistic aspects of *Twilight Princess* that helped to bring certain players back to the series after the more childlike orientation of the GameCube installment. On the other hand, while *The Wind Waker* managed to make a place for itself by drawing as many defenders as detractors of the decision to bring a cartoon-like art style to the franchise, later episodes in the same category (*Phantom Hourglass*, *Spirit Tracks*, *Four Swords Adventures*, *Triforce Heroes*) had far less of an impact. In other words, it's generally agreed that the gaming public mostly prefers the more "mature" *Zelda* episodes. Even so, it's only fair to acknowledge that *The Wind Waker*'s cartoon style has aged much better than the episodes that adopted a more realistic art style. Even a cursory comparison of the HD remasters of *The Wind Waker* and *Twilight Princess* for the Wii U is enough to realize how dated the latter looks, while the former looks as fresh as the day it came out. And yet, the original versions of these games were released a full four years apart.

But this debate seems to have become increasingly irrelevant in recent years. Since the release of *Skyward Sword*, in fact, the question is rarely raised in any serious way, and no one is particularly shocked by this change in attitude. Should we conclude that the artistic direction in that episode, which was neither too mature nor too childish, struck just the right balance to satisfy both groups of fans and put an end to the debate? And indeed, *Breath of the Wild* didn't set off any passionate arguments about its art style when it was released either, as if the creators of the series had once again managed to find a compromise that everyone could agree on. While there's certainly nothing excessively "mature" about the art direction in the new *Zelda* episode, it still reflects the visual ambivalence of a world that can swing from deadly violence to dreamlike wonder in the blink of an eye without threatening the game's consistent overall tone. Once again, it's all a matter of balance. But perhaps more problematic for some players than the visual style of *The Wind Waker* was the choice to make Link himself a child in that game. However, since Link is clearly an adult in both *Skyward Sword* and *Breath of the Wild*, we can consider this discussion to be closed.

A NEW LINK

THE BENEFITS OF AMNESIA

Up until *Breath of the Wild*, whether consciously or not, the creators of *The Legend of Zelda* always presented Link's character according to the same logic: the idea of constructing the hero's own legend in the present moment. Through the young Hylian's actions, players are irresistibly guided to assemble the pieces of a narrative puzzle over which they have no control, but which will ultimately allow them to achieve Link's destiny and forge his legend. Whether he's traveling in a parallel dimension (*A Link to the Past*, *Twilight Princess*), through time (*Ocarina of Time*), in dreams (*Link's Awakening*), or in a world of the infinitesimally small (*The Minish Cap*), the player must be able to experience the same things as the character they embody, discover Link's adventure at the same time as he does, and make his story their own.

For all of these reasons, Link has always been presented as an empty shell, an anonymous hero that we can name however we like and who never says anything so that each of us can imagine ourselves in his place. He is not the sort of hero who has a complex and fully-developed psychological profile that we can gradually come to understand by examining his past actions one by one. At most, his reactions to certain situations allow us to imagine Link as something of an introvert, a bit on the shy side, but also as someone who will stop at nothing to defend humanity's most noble values. And even that is only one subjective interpretation among others that has to be adjusted in light of various unusual situations that arise in different episodes of the saga. For example, his mischievous side comes out for players who choose to play him as a sneaky thief in the store from *Link's Awakening*. Not nearly as bland and featureless a character as many observers tend to describe him, we also see an unexpectedly facetious or even insolent side of Link's personality in *Breath of the Wild* in certain rather impolite dialogue options included to surprise and amuse the player.

Beyond this one tiny detail, the game actually contains plenty of other hints that seem to indicate that Link's personality has changed. The hero who awakens in *Breath of the Wild* after a century-long slumber is not the man we expected to encounter. Stripped of his green tunic and his iconic cap, the young Hylian bears almost no visual resemblance at all to the Link we once knew. He is now right-handed instead of left-handed, and the player has no option to customize his name. And most importantly, he has amnesia. It's at this point that we realize that the creative process that brought the Link of *Breath of the Wild* into the world has nothing to do with the hero from the other installments in the series. While the protagonist in the earlier adventures was actively building his own legend in the present moment, his journey in *Breath of the Wild* is all about reconstructing his past. No longer is Link writing a new page of his history with each of the game's major story beats; instead, our hero finds himself in a situation where he no longer knows who he is and in which the adventure itself has no meaning until the player finds a way to help him get his memory back. This approach is all too familiar to RPG fans and is often seen as a bit of a cop-out: relying on the hero's amnesia to justify the fact that the player knows nothing of the backstory at the start of the adventure, while ensuring that their progression through the game will help them put the pieces back together. Placed on an equal footing, the player and their avatar are both motivated to cut through the shroud of mystery around their lost past, thereby revealing the keys to understanding the plot. For as we've already seen, collecting Link's fragmented memories may not be strictly required in *Breath of the Wild*, but it is the only way to understand the deep connections that tie the hero to the people responsible for the present situation, most of whom he will probably never see again.

With this approach, *Breath of the Wild* risks leaving players with a sense of *déjà vu* by turning to one of the industry's most classic formulas (heroes with amnesia have appeared in *Final Fantasy VII*, *BioShock*, and *Red Dead Redemption*, among others), but there are good reasons behind this decision. In the April 2017 issue of *EDGE* magazine, director Hidemaro Fujibayashi explains that the choice to give Link amnesia was directly related to the game's open world structure. While obviously not intended as an innovative move, since countless earlier titles have also used this device, the decision grew out of a desire to incorporate the open world gameplay into the narrative structure itself. Putting the player in control of a hero who wakes up in the middle of nowhere with no idea of what he is supposed to do is a fine way to learn how the player will go about finding answers to the many questions they have. What's most interesting about this approach is that the totally free structure of an open world game allows for a virtually infinite number of possibilities. Fujibayashi emphasizes the importance of placing the player and the character on the same level: "What would you do if you were in this situation? How would you go about finding out who you are and what's happening around you? The answer to these questions could be the solution for an approach based on discovering a rich story in a world as open as this one." So in fact, there's not just one correct answer, but an infinite number of solutions. This is how the use of an open world design justifies the choice of a fragmented narrative structure based on collecting memories. Each of Link's memories allows him to gain a slightly better understanding of what's happening and what the others expect of him, but he's never required to follow a specific path. On that note, it would be intriguing—and quite revealing—to compare the paths by which different players explore the world of Hyrule during their time with *Breath of the Wild*. And in fact, that's exactly what the Hero's Path mode, included in the DLC released on June 30, 2017, allows us to do: to see on the world map precisely where each player has traveled in their last two hundred hours in the game. It seems safe to assume that the geometric shapes traced out by these paths will be very different from one player to the next.

ANOTHER WAY OF TURNING THE PAGE?

Our first volume of *Zelda: The History of a Legendary Saga* included an extensive analysis of how Link's character had evolved over the series, especially in the pivotal episode *Ocarina of Time*. That discussion highlighted a certain number of symbolic elements that we will briefly return to here in order to demonstrate how far the creative process around Link in *Breath of the Wild* has moved away from them.

We saw in that book that the franchise had always remained faithful to the ways it chose to present its main character, from the first *Zelda* game right up to *Skyward Sword* almost thirty years later. The main idea was to never go too far in filling out Link's personality, in order to make it as easy as possible for any player to identify with the hero. Besides intentionally distancing itself in this way from the many titles that gave their protagonists detailed psychological profiles with little room for players to provide their own interpretations, *Zelda* also treated each of its stories as a kind of trial for the hero. In each of his various adventures and especially in *Ocarina of Time*, Link generally started with some sort of initiation process (quest for medallions) that led to his induction into a new state (acquiring the legendary sword, entering adulthood) before finally beginning his true spiritual journey. Each dungeon that he fought his way through symbolized a period of isolation in which the hero assimilated newly-learned skills that then allowed him to continue with his moral transformation. As in a traditional rite of passage, his voyage unfolded along the path proposed by an omniscient instructor: the owl. Like a mythical guide whose role was to accompany the souls of the deceased to their new home, the owl had only to turn his head to evoke another symbolic meaning—the idea of clairvoyance. This approach, in conjunction with the main character's presentation as an "empty shell" to be filled with each player's individual interpretations, aimed to establish a close parallel between Link's own progress and that of the player who controlled him. Ultimately, Link symbolized the hero who supposedly resides within each of us, and his true nature was defined not by his past, but by the legend created over the course of each episode.

In *Breath of the Wild*, the process of reconstructing the hero's past in hopes of curing his amnesia puts the game on a completely different track. For the first time in the series, the goal is no longer to experience a story through Link's eyes, but to reconstruct the puzzle of his identity by collecting lost memories that are essential to understanding his quest. The only real commonality that we might attempt to establish between these two approaches lies in the near-personification of Hyrule Castle. In the analysis presented in our first volume, we concluded that the castle was treated as a character in its own right, rather than simply a part of the scenery. And in *Breath of the Wild*, as in *Ocarina of Time*, the enemy's corruption of this sacred place leads to a perception of Hyrule Castle as a reflection of the darkness that secretly lurks deep in Link's own heart. The nightmarish silhouette that engulfs the castle in darkness is a metaphorical representation—or even a literal one, since it's heavily inspired by Ganon's final form in *Ocarina of Time*—of a primitive evil that has endured for centuries.

Despite this new perspective which departs from earlier episodes in the series, we never get the sense that *Breath of the Wild* is working to dismantle its predecessors' legacy. As producer Eiji Aonuma hinted in a January 2017 interview with the French website *Gamekult*, Link's latest adventure doesn't contradict the spirit that has defined the series since the beginning: "While we were talking [during a promotional tour in New York], Miyamoto-san found the perfect way of expressing it: the essence of the *Legend of Zelda* is an environment in which Link can evolve and grow stronger, in ways that players can feel directly through the different actions he's able to take over the course of the story."

So while each of us may have formed our own personal opinions over the years about what constitutes the essence of the *Zelda* franchise, it will have to adapt to fit with the experience we encounter in *Breath of the Wild*, however unique and unexpected it may be.

THE FOURTH WALL

THE ULTIMATE GAME DESIGN TRICK

Originally drawn from the vocabulary of the stage, the idea of "breaking the fourth wall" in dramatic work has inspired many forms of expression in different media over the years. Whatever "language" a given work may use (theater, literature, movies, TV series, graphic novels, video games, etc.), the common thread here is that the work breaks free of the limits that are supposed to define it by directly addressing the person experiencing it. Though safe and sound behind their book or TV screen or hidden in the shadows among the seats of the theater, readers or viewers suddenly realize that they are not as untouchable or inaccessible as they thought—a realization that rattles their most fundamental assumptions. By addressing its audience directly or indirectly, the work extends its reach into the world of those who had thought that they could simply admire it from afar and practically invites them to jump in and play a role.

In its original theatrical meaning, the idea of the "fourth wall" refers to the imaginary barrier that separates the stage from the audience—and explodes into tiny pieces when an actor speaks to a viewer or when some aspect of the play creates a direct link to the audience and demands an immediate reaction. This technique suddenly establishes an interaction between the two sides of the "wall"—ideally just at the moment when viewers are least expecting it, thus ensuring their complete surprise. The lack of separation creates the illusion of being directly visible to an actor or fictional character who is suddenly acting as if they can really see us—yes, "us," the viewers in the front row or looking at the screen, the reader turning the pages or the player who thought they were invisible behind their controller. Depending on how the fourth wall is broken, we may feel that the character talking to us is fully aware of their status as a fictional character, like the antihero Deadpool who knows perfectly well that he exists only in the pages of a comic book and regularly points this out—to the utter confusion of the other characters around him. In other cases, only the viewer can hear what the character is saying, like the title character in the TV series *Malcolm in the Middle*, who speaks to us as though we were right there next to him.

While there are no shortage of examples in movies and TV series, this technique has also made its mark in the world of video games—and there's a good reason why the *Metal Gear Solid* franchise is so often cited for its clever ways of breaking the fourth wall. While plenty of other titles have made brilliant use of the concept (*Baten Kaitos*, *The Nomad Soul*, *Eternal Darkness*, *The Stanley Parable*, and many more), Hideo Kojima's work is almost universally seen as the most effective example of this technique, with the creator doing everything in his power to bewilder and confuse players by creating the illusion that, rather than controlling the game, they are in fact being controlled by it. In the first *Metal Gear Solid* game, Kojima cleverly turns the tables by showing us that we can interact with the game in more ways than simply pressing buttons on the controller. For example, when we face off against the boss Psycho Mantis, who can read our mind and move objects near us by telekinesis, we quickly feel a pang of doubt. The illusion is so effective that we actually find ourselves wondering how this virtual villain could possibly know what our favorite games are and guess whether we are cautious or bold by nature. His ability to read our thoughts also makes it impossible to try and fight him in the usual way. But it turns out that the trick is based on simply reading the memory card that contains all our game data (including whether we've played other Konami games and the number of times we've saved our game) and on the vibration function of the PlayStation's DualShock controller. By anticipating our actions, Kojima imposes his own interpretation on them, encouraging us to think differently about video games by looking for solutions in our own reality—on our side of the infamous fourth wall. In the end, neutralizing Psycho Mantis's psychic abilities requires us to plug our controller into a different port so that the boss can no longer detect which buttons we're pressing. Through his games and especially in the *Metal Gear* franchise (including the stunning conclusion of *MGS 2* and the trick that lets us avoid fighting The End in *MGS 3*), Kojima uses and abuses these game design tricks to trip us up by interfering in our own reality.

More recently, the surprising *NieR: Automata* also includes a certain number of narrative twists that force the player to question themselves throughout the game—but we won't spoil the surprise by discussing them here. The ultimate high point is the crisis of conscience we face during the interactive closing credits (ending E), over a soaring musical theme with a message of hope and altruism entitled *Weight of the World*. Proof enough that the unpredictable Taro Yoko is no less brilliant than his compatriot Hideo Kojima!

DOES *ZELDA* BREAK THE FOURTH WALL?

Faced with this level of mischief and ingenuity at squeezing every drop of excitement from the idea of the fourth wall, *Breath of the Wild* wisely declines to directly challenge the true masters of the technique. But it does make a pointed allusion to it in its opening moments. The first few minutes of the game, in which Link awakens from a hundred-year slumber, immediately grab our attention. Through her words, Princess Zelda seems to be addressing both the hero and the player, and this impression is reinforced when we acquire the Sheikah Slate a moment later. As we have already explained at length, the design of this essential item in *Breath of the Wild* intentionally evokes the look of the Gamepad controller for Wii U, the console for which the game was originally designed, and the similarity is no coincidence. As Link takes possession of the slate, the player sees their own controller react in more or less the same way, giving them the feeling of being in the same situation as the character they're controlling. Although this initial aspect loses much of its punch in the Switch version of the game, we can still sense the desire to establish the Sheikah Slate as a concrete link between the player and their avatar, creating a sort of recursive "hall of mirrors" effect.

Repeated like a litany in a few of the trailers released to promote the game, Zelda's words ("*Open your eyes!*") reminded many viewers of how the same phrase was used in Cameron Crowe's *Vanilla Sky*, the American remake of the Spanish film *Abre los ojos* (i.e. "open your eyes") directed by Alejandro Amenábar. In both cases, we're unsure whether the protagonist will be saved or traumatized by opening his eyes. Both stories are also mainly presented through flashbacks and various leaps forward and backward in time. But most importantly, *Breath of the Wild* comes full circle at the end of the game when Princess Zelda asks, "Do you remember me?"—and her question seems aimed squarely at the player, rather than at Link. Behind this deceptively ordinary question lies an implicit reference to our mission to collect hidden memories from all over the world. Through the young woman's question as to whether we have found all the hidden flashbacks, the designers of *Breath of the Wild* urge us one last time not to stop at simply finishing the story, but to make an extra effort to better understand it. After all, this hunt for hundred-year-old memories is the only way to learn even a bit more about the mysterious princess of whom we see so little if we limit ourselves to taking the quickest path through the game. In terms of pure completionism, finishing the quest for the captured memories is also the only way to access the game's "real" ending, presented as a bonus sequence after the credits. In it, we see Zelda telling Link of her plan to do everything she can to help rebuild the kingdom, thus adding a note of hope and positivity to the initial ending. So in the end, it's Princess Zelda herself whose words invite us to solve the ultimate mystery behind our adventure.

With all this in mind, we can see that *Breath of the Wild* breaks the fourth wall in its own relatively discreet way, with no attempt to shock or surprise the player. The process here is quite distinct from the other examples we mentioned earlier, with the main purpose being to remind the player through the virtual protagonist of their quest's hidden goal. As such, the approach is different from what we might have expected, but still represents a relatively rare move for the series, even though previous *Zelda* games had also tried to speak to players through the fourth wall. On the DS, the episode *The Legend of Zelda: Phantom Hourglass* used a memorable trick borrowed from the inventive *Another Code* by featuring a puzzle that could only be solved by folding the console's dual screen shut to make a map appear. It's just one more way for a video game to flip the script for a moment and turn the player into a mere puppet in the hands of mischievous developers.

Through its narrative design and its heavy emphasis on the memory fragments, which are the only real way to fully understand the story as a whole, *Breath of the Wild* also seems to be trying to confront players with their own memories of the saga. It's as if the game wanted to focus our attention on the past—not just within its own story, but on the past history of the franchise itself and our own history as fans. But why? Probably in order to highlight the shared heritage between the series and the people who have enjoyed it as players. In fact, this is an extension of the hypothesis we presented in the first volume of *Zelda: The History of a Legendary Saga* about the meaning behind one of the key scenes in *The Wind Waker*: the moment when we discover what used to be the kingdom of Hyrule, swallowed up by the ocean waves and frozen in a past seen in black and white. By presenting *Ocarina of Time* as a sacred legend through the use of stained-glass windows relating the Hero of Time's exploits, Eiji Aonuma (who had just recently taken charge of the franchise) seemed to be paying homage to the brilliant and mythical legacy left by Shigeru Miyamoto. And by casting Link in *The Wind Waker* as an innocent child who was clearly never intended to push the hero of *Ocarina of Time* out of the special place he held in fans' hearts, was Aonuma perhaps signaling that he himself still had a lot to learn before earning his place as the spiritual successor to his "master Miyamoto"?

By analogy, when we look at the parallels established between the two time periods in *Breath of the Wild*, we can see much the same desire to evoke a past history (which the player has not experienced this time) in order to use it not as a humble statement of inferiority, but as a concrete illustration of his newfound maturity as the producer of the series. The hero may have failed a century ago, but when he awakens in the present, he is ready to prevail. In other words, the Link we see in the past seems to represent the younger Eiji Aonuma, overwhelmed by the towering legacy of *Ocarina of Time* and unable to match its achievements, while Link in the present symbolizes the fruit of his mature efforts, namely *Breath of the Wild* itself, with which he may be about to surpass that very legacy.

PROMISES KEPT?

As Eiji Aonuma regularly pointed out, with game design choices as ambitious as those made in *Breath of the Wild*, the whole team had to throw themselves body and soul into a development process that was intentionally time-consuming and meticulous. As enormous as it was risky, their task obviously led to great commercial and critical success. But did they really keep all of the promises that were made at the start of the project?

DOES THE ART DIRECTION MAKE UP FOR SUBPAR GRAPHICS?

Well before anyone had actually gotten their hands on a copy of *Breath of the Wild*, the game had already been subjected to sarcastic criticism from observers whose main takeaway from the earliest trailers was the substandard visual quality of a game that was supposed to be the flagship title for the new

Nintendo Switch. These critics may have forgotten that, on the one hand, the game had not been designed to maximize the capacities of the new console, since it was originally intended for development on the Wii U—and more importantly, that Nintendo's reputation was never primarily based on the visual aspect of its games.

Though perhaps less flagrantly than *The Wind Waker* and *Skyward Sword* before it, *Breath of the Wild* also chose to construct a unique visual identity with an art direction that ran counter to the constant search for greater realism seen in other productions. Everything about the character design, the choice of environments, and the animations for living creatures conspires to give the game a "high fantasy" look that sometimes approaches that of an animated film. But the graphics quality is still realistic enough to avoid reproducing the almost childlike outlines that proved so controversial in *The Wind Waker*, as appropriate for the more dramatic themes of this episode. As a result, there are plenty of moments in the adventure when we are struck by just how effective this artistic direction can be, located just at the boundary between the real and the imaginary. Discovering mystical items and locations has an even more powerful impact in contrast to the perfectly believable look of most of the world's basic features. In the chapter about nature's central role in the game, we already mentioned a few of the likely influences that may have inspired the art team in the creative process that led to some of the game's more fantastic and dreamlike elements. We can clearly sense a deep fascination and profound respect for the works of Studio Ghibli (*Nausicaä of the Valley of the Wind*, *Princess Mononoke*) in the animations of the dragons that wriggle their way across the sky and the sometimes surreal wildlife that embodies the spirit of ancient nature. And let's not forget the wild horses who move with such grace that time seems to stand still whenever we stop to admire them. Whether conscious or not, it's this influence from the most noble and poetic aspects of Japanese animation that give *Breath of the Wild* the sense of mystical wonder that it needed to remind us that the world we are exploring is the fruit of someone's imagination. In this sense, even if certain technical shortcomings lead to a less than fully realistic look, this in no way compromises the thrilling immersion we feel when galloping over the plains at breakneck speed or soaring through an endless sky with our paraglider.

Nintendo never promised us breathtaking graphics and, indeed, the company has always clearly preferred to focus its energy on enriching the gameplay experience, even to the detriment of other aspects. As it happens, the team behind the new *Zelda* game had plenty of occasions to justify their choices. For example, in an article published on the French site *Jeuxvideo.com* in late January of 2017, producer Eiji Aonuma explained that the use of an animation-like style allowed the team to reuse certain visual elements from the development of *The*

Wind Waker. Although both of the games have their own completely distinct feel, Nintendo's experience on the most cartoon-like of the *Zelda* games made the development process easier for *Breath of the Wild* by allowing the team to build on existing visual assets in a way that is ultimately invisible to the player. In any case, as Aonuma noted in an interview with *LeMonde.fr* at around the same time, the visual style was never intended as a tribute to *The Wind Waker*, but resulted from a clear-eyed game design decision: "Since we have this really, really huge world in *Breath of the Wild*, a simplified drawing style means that the objectives you have to reach will be much more legible and visible. And of course, as you can imagine, all of our artists were raised on Japanese animation, so this visual style is one of our strengths and part of what gives Japanese games their identity." In short, the intentional similarities with Japanese animation in general also allowed the developers to build on past accomplishments and turn them into an additional asset.

In the last "making of" video, released by Nintendo in March 2017 and featuring various anecdotes from the team leads about what happened behind the scenes during the development process, artistic director Satoru Takizawa reminds us that the goal was not to prioritize graphics performance or realism above all else, but to make the game fun to play. In *Breath of the Wild*, as in almost every Nintendo game, the art design was carefully selected to support the underlying gameplay. Satoru Takizawa explains it as follows: "Of course, as the team in charge of the graphic design, we wanted to produce gorgeous and realistic landscapes, but what we most tried to keep in mind was making all of those visual elements work with the details of the gameplay so that the user would feel more comfortable while playing. So when we had to choose between making the game look prettier or improving the feel of the gameplay, we always prioritized the gameplay aspects. I hope that players will be able to appreciate the world on their own, beyond whatever videos they may have seen." For example, it turns out that Ganon's appearance in *Breath of the Wild* was initially defined in terms of the gameplay sequence that the team had worked out for the final boss and later adjusted to fit with the overall aesthetic of the world. This rule was not always applied in exactly the same way, however, as we see in the case of Princess Zelda, whose design primarily grew out of the artistic director's idea of the role that her character would play in the game. In general, the graphic design for any of the game's main characters had to be approved by the director, the producer, and by Shigeru Miyamoto himself. In light of all this, it's then up to each of us to evaluate for ourselves whether the idea of consistently subordinating the visual design to gameplay comfort was a successful approach or not.

DOES BREATH OF THE WILD REDEFINE THE NOTION OF AN OPEN WORLD?

Although it certainly improved the game's quality in many ways, was all the energy spent on this first open world *Zelda* game really enough to refresh the very idea of what an open world game can do, as many observers had hoped? The question is actually larger than it seems, and it would probably be foolish to try giving a complete answer before a few years have passed to see what kind of impact this game will have on those that come after it. What's already clear, though, is that by smashing all the locks that had kept most games in the genre from achieving complete freedom, Nintendo had opened a breach for all the creative minds who saw open world games as a vast field of possibilities in which existing games had only begun to scratch the surface. We won't take the time here to revisit all the unique aspects of its game design that made *Breath of the Wild* stand out in a category that it had never really ventured into before, but let us simply observe that what makes the game so fascinating as a whole is how effectively all of its different ideas fit together. Although the formula used here includes many obvious influences from the most widely respected open world games, this episode of the *Zelda* saga deserves credit for its exceptionally inventive ability to put its own spin on conventions that had previously been completely foreign to it. The elements that most effectively convey a feeling of freedom and exploration, like the paraglider and unrestricted climbing, quickly established themselves as indispensable features of the game—so they'll probably start showing up in new titles from Nintendo's competitors as well. But what makes *Breath of the Wild* such a success is also its mastery of space and its amazing knack for finding the most effective tricks to transform what could have been a dull and repetitive experience into a constant voyage of discovery filled with countless secrets and quests. Players have such a wide variety of approaches to completing their adventure that the experience never feels routine, even after a hundred hours or more in the game. Because each of its building blocks is part of the same unfailingly logical and consistent system, what really drives our interest in the game is the desire to experiment with the subtleties of its gameplay beyond what even seems possible at first.

From this point of view, we would argue that this form of absolute freedom was probably what the series had been missing in its efforts to renew itself and break free of its archaic linear routines.

But there is one aspect directly related to the open world structure that the designers of *Breath of the Wild* couldn't quite get a handle on: the difficulty level. By deciding to give players free access to the four main dungeons once they've collected all the runes (by completing the first four Shrines on the Great Plateau), the designers ran the risk of creating an imbalance with the gradual increase in the player's strength and abilities. Extremely vulnerable at the start of the game, our character is confronted with dangers far out of proportion to the resources available to him, regardless of the specific path he takes. Of course, we have access to enough survival tricks in *Breath of the Wild* to scrape by, but the first few hours of the game are nonetheless challenging, and death comes frequently when we have just three hearts in our health meter and are still getting used to the gameplay, leaving very little room for error.

On the other hand, the more trials we overcome, the more health and stamina our avatar accumulates, until he is eventually almost too well-prepared for the final dungeons to even feel like a proper challenge. Not only can we extend our health meter by exploring the many Shrines hidden throughout the world, but we can also upgrade our equipment by acquiring powerful weapons and by going to the Great Fairies to reinforce our armor. Soon, death becomes a much less frequent occurrence, and the trials required to access the dungeons and make our way through them start to seem like a walk in the park, not to mention how weak the bosses are. In other words, no matter what path we choose to take through the adventure, we can't help noticing a distinct imbalance between the start and the end of our journey. The difficulty level is not progressive, but static, and our bitter struggles in the first few hours give way to a sense of coasting through the final stretch, right where we'd normally expect to face the game's most epic challenges.

To be fair, allowing players to go directly to any of the four dungeons meant that the designers had to make it possible to get through them with limited resources and the minimum number of hearts. As a result, once we start to power up a bit, the game no longer pushes us to the limits of our ability. This imbalance becomes all the more obvious if we decide not to take on the four Divine Beasts until our hero's development is well underway, say after fifty hours or so in the game, with fifteen hearts in our health meter and a well-stocked inventory of weapons and armor.

In light of all this, we can perhaps see the limitations of the decision to rely on a constant level of difficulty to offer a viable overall experience in the context of an open world. Whereas earlier *Zelda* games excelled at providing a progressive challenge that constantly adapted to our abilities, *Breath of the Wild* demands every ounce of our effort at the start of the game, then leaves us with the sense that we're speeding through its later challenges. In this sense, we don't get to benefit from Nintendo's usual perfect mastery of game design and level design in this episode, since the developers can no longer reliably build these elements around specific assumptions about the player's level of experience. Of course, we can each come to our own conclusions about how much of a problem this is, but it certainly represents one of the most radical changes in the history of the series.

OTHER THINGS WE WOULD HAVE LIKED TO SEE

Even when they get top scores from critics, which isn't all that rare in the world of video games, no one would claim that even the most spectacular games are truly perfect. *Breath of the Wild* is no exception, of course, and has its share of imperfections too, even beyond its technical limitations and certain gameplay choices that were not always well-received.

One obvious example is the fragmented narrative that results from Link's amnesia—a story that we can only reconstruct by assembling the puzzle of his lost memories. While the idea seems appealing at first, in practice it turns out to be relatively frustrating for the player. Unless we're willing to constantly turn aside from our main objective to roam every corner of the world looking for these fragments of the past, we are forced to accept that we will never have all the keys we need to understand the story as a whole.

Princess Zelda, meanwhile, is more inaccessible than ever. We only see her in the distant past, in flashbacks that are far too brief for players to really feel like we've gotten to know this tormented young woman. The same is true of the four great Champions whose different personalities we would have loved to learn more about, and who manage to breathe life into the past century all by themselves, while the present day seems so lackluster in comparison. So it's no surprise to learn that the second DLC for *Breath of the Wild*—entitled *The Champions' Ballad* in reference to a song by Kass the troubadour and released at the end of 2017—does focus on their story.

Many players felt that, as bold and innovative as they may be, the new dungeons designed around the ability to rotate and rearrange them through terminals controlled by the player still aren't enough to make up for the loss of "real" dungeons like the ones in earlier episodes. There has been a lot of debate over whether and how *Breath of the Wild* might have included temples designed like the ones for which the series first became known. Although the overall approach of the new game doesn't seem like an ideal match for long explorations in enclosed spaces, it would still have been exciting to get at least one small sample for nostalgia's sake—even if it meant reducing the truly excessive number of hidden Shrines in the game (need we remind you that there are hundred and twenty of them?). Multi-level dungeons made up of multiple rooms combining puzzles and skirmishes with enemies might well have been a worthwhile addition to the adventure.

Let's also recall what producer Eiji Aonuma said in the Nintendo Direct broadcast of January 23, 2013, even before any details of *Breath of the Wild* had been revealed. As part of the process of rethinking the series' basic conventions, he mentioned the idea of adapting to modern players' expectations by surprising them in various ways. He referred to "the fact that the player expects to have to finish the dungeons in a certain order or the fact that they'll be playing alone." While the first point seems to have been handled with panache in *Breath of the Wild*, it's still not clear what he meant by the second.

But the producer provided a partial answer in the final "making of" video released by Nintendo in March 2017. Aonuma explained that this episode had been designed to let players share the game with friends, unlike earlier episodes in the series which were intended to be played alone (except, of course, for multiplayer installments like *Four Swords* or *Tri Force Heroes*). Even if only one person is controlling the player, the game was designed to encourage cooperation, since anyone can easily jump in to offer their ideas on how to get past this or that difficulty. Since progress in the game is mainly based on experimentation, spectators can also get involved in the game by suggesting new things to try or new paths to explore. Aonuma ended his comments by saying that he intended to play with his children to experience their reactions as part of a fun and interactive gaming session—and that even if the Nintendo Switch tends to encourage a single-player experience in its handheld mode, he hoped that players would also get together with friends and family around the television from time to time to enjoy this kind of communication as they play.

From this point of view, the producer believes that *Breath of the Wild* succeeds in breaking the norms of the franchise once again by offering a new kind of gaming experience that can be shared with others. We leave it to the reader to decide whether this idea fulfills Aonuma's initial promise that players would no longer have to play alone or whether he might have been hinting at a multiplayer option that was part of the original plan but ultimately abandoned.

Of course, alongside everything we would have liked to see in *Breath of the Wild*, there's also the unfortunate fact that not all of the core gameplay elements are equally effective. For example, many players find that the changes made to the melee system have led to a less enjoyable combat experience than in the other 3D episodes. The main problem is that the lock function for targeting enemies is not sufficiently optimized when it comes to reflexively dodging enemy attacks, which can now involve any number of different weapons with widely varying ranges and speeds. In fact, although the combat system is still quite solid and convincing overall, the sense of disappointment mainly comes from the fact that one of the best parts of *Ocarina of Time* for the Nintendo 64 was its perfect implementation of "Z-targeting," the lock function that allowed for spontaneous and highly effective counterattacks. In *Breath of the Wild*, however, this same lock function almost makes combat harder.

Although this is just one example among others, it shows that this game cannot claim to be better than its legendary predecessors on every single point. Any major change to a game's overall orientation involves more or less serious consequences for its various individual aspects, and those consequences are not always easy to anticipate or to correct. Far from infallible, *Breath of the Wild* does not claim to be better than the episodes that came before it, but it does try to do things differently.

ZELDA

THE HISTORY OF A LEGENDARY SAGA
VOLUME 2: BREATH OF THE WILD

CONCLUSION

IS *BREATH OF THE WILD* A "REAL" *ZELDA* GAME?

HEN playing *Breath of the Wild*, any long-time fan of the *Legend of Zelda* series will naturally tend to ask themselves: do I feel like I'm playing a "real" *Zelda* game? It's a legitimate question, in light of all the changes to the gameplay system that ultimately led back to the cutting-edge open world formula introduced thirty years ago in the first installment in the series. Of course, our answers to this question will necessarily be somewhat subjective, since each of us has our own very personal understanding of what the franchise means to us. To understand just how tricky it is to decide whether a given episode deserves to be seen as a "real" *Zelda* game, especially if we base our judgment solely on criteria relating to game design, consider the example of *Zelda II: The Adventure of Link*. While *The Adventure of Link* contains far too many changes to the core formula to be considered as representative of the series, it's still seen as a great game by a certain fringe group of players who couldn't imagine the franchise without this unusual episode.

By analogy, would anyone claim that *Breath of the Wild* is too different from its predecessors to deserve a place in the family tree? Certainly not, especially if we think back to the rudimentary open world that was sketched out in the first *Zelda* game and the almost nostalgic way in which *Breath of the Wild* leads us back to it. Of course, the tools used today are more modern and the world is several orders of magnitude larger, but the approach is still similar, with the same desire to let players take control of their own adventure from start to finish. In his January 2017 interview with the French site *Jeuxvideo.com*, producer Eiji Aonuma had already addressed this central question directly in hopes of reassuring worried fans: "We designed this *Zelda* game as a *Zelda* game—in an open world, yes, but most importantly, as a *Zelda* game."

From that point forward, the tools put in place to develop the game's world and allow us to explore it are ultimately of secondary importance. What counts is not that almost everything about this *Zelda* episode is different from the other installments in the series, but that each of the new ideas implemented here is essentially an extension of some specific key component of the series.

Our ability to explore the world of *Breath of the Wild* in complete freedom may seem to be in contrast with the linear structure of earlier episodes, but it reflects a goal that the creators had been striving to achieve since the beginning. Nintendo may have gone back to the drawing board for the designs of the dungeons that we're asked to explore, but the puzzles and the combat that characterized the old-school dungeons are still omnipresent in their own way throughout the game. And after all, even the episodes in which Princess Zelda fails to appear—even though her name is right there in the title—have never had their status as "real" *Zelda* games called into question. Somewhat paradoxically, one such episode, *Link's Awakening*, is even a fan favorite.

From its creators' point of view, in any case, *Breath of the Wild* seems to embody the new face of the franchise, to judge by Eiji Aonuma's comments on the saga's immediate future. Within a few years, Nintendo has every intention of giving its new Switch console a *Zelda* game designed specifically for that platform, and the resounding success of *Breath of the Wild* seems very likely to influence the general orientation of the next episode's game design. How similar will this new Switch-exclusive *Zelda* game be to its predecessor in terms of its open world design, atmosphere, and story? No one can answer that yet. But since it's highly unlikely that Nintendo's teams will give up trying to surprise us and just serve up the same old ideas warmed over, it's safe to assume that the next installment will also find its own ways to redefine what should be considered a "real" *Zelda* game.

In any case, it's clear that no one could have predicted that the release of *The Legend of Zelda: Breath of the Wild* would meet with such sincere enthusiasm and excitement from players all over the world. Nintendo's decision to take the boldest possible risks by completely rethinking the foundations of its wildly popular series was apparently the only way to jump-start real change for a franchise that had resisted it for far too long and that was starting to raise serious concerns for its community of dedicated fans. Besides the courage of the publisher, the producer, and the director, the whole team that worked on developing this new title deserves credit for their amazing achievement in succeeding where so many others had failed. For unlike other licenses that have never questioned their own basic conventions or that have simply fallen into decline as they age (*Mass Effect*, *Assassin's Creed*, etc.), *The Legend of Zelda* has already shown its ability to reclaim the aura of prestige that had eluded it for far too many years—an achievement that seems all the more poignant when we consider how long it's been since video game fans got this excited about a new episode in the saga.

ZELDA

THE HISTORY OF A LEGENDARY SAGA

VOLUME 2: BREATH OF THE WILD

AUTHOR'S
ACKNOWLEDGMENTS

Thanks to Nicolas Courcier and Mehdi El Kanafi for their confidence in me, for the unique opportunity they gave me to write about *Zelda*, and for many enlightening discussions around the process of writing this book.

To the creators of *The Legend of Zelda* for introducing us all to a myth that will continue to inspire generations of players for many years to come.

To my family and friends for their constant support and encouragement.

To Damien, for taking the time to read and check over the chapter on music in *Breath of the Wild*.

To Camille, Korok radar and champion go player. Ogata had better hang on tight! Thanks for the improvised co-op in the Joy-Con riding trials.

To Graphite and Balezane, whose cuddles I'm already missing; and to Stella, the "legendary mare" who's every bit as epic as Epona.

To everyone who supports our publications here at Third Éditions, in ways both big and small, and to everyone who helps create them.

ZELDA

THE HISTORY OF A LEGENDARY SAGA
VOLUME 2: BREATH OF THE WILD

BIBLIOGRAPHY

PUBLISHED WORKS:

Zelda. The History of a Legendary Saga, Volume 1 (Third Editions).
Hyrule Historia (Dark Horse Books).
Zelda Arts & Artifacts (artbook, for the interview at the end of the book).
EDGE, April 2017 issue, including a section on *Zelda: Breath of the Wild.*
Special issue of French magazine *The Game: Les Cahiers de la Playhistoire Spécial Zelda.*

WEBSITES:

http://zelda.com/online-guide
http://zelda.gamepedia.com
http://zelda.wikia.com/wiki/Zeldapedia
http://fr.zelda.wikia.com/wiki/ZeldaWiki
http://www.zeldadungeon.net/wiki

INTERVIEWS AND REPORTS:

GDC session: "Change and Constant: Breaking Conventions with *The Legend of Zelda: Breath of the Wild*" by the creators of the game: *https://www.youtube. com/ watch?v=QyMsF31NdNc*

http://www.lemonde.fr/pixels/article/2017/03/03/conception-de-zelda-breath-of-the-wild-un-prototype-en-2d-un-biker-et-des-extraterrestres_5088655_4408996.html

All the Nintendo Direct broadcasts relating to the game.

The three official "making of" videos: *https://www.nintendo.fr/News/2017/Mars/ Decouvrez-les-coulisses-de-la-realisation-de-The-Legend-of-Zelda-Breath-of-the- Wild-1206592.html*

http://kotaku.com/when-miyamoto-first-played-zelda-breath-of-the- wild-h-1793017234

https://www.theverge.com/2017/3/7/14830152/nintendo-legend-of-zelda-director- interview-death-challenge-design

https://www.theverge.com/2017/3/11/14881076/the-legend-of-zelda-breath-of-the- wild-nintendo-interview

http://www.gameblog.fr/news/65774-rencontre-avec-eiji-aonuma-zelda-breath- of-the-wild-nintendo

http://www.jeuxvideo.com/videos/chroniques/599335/zelda-breath-of-the-wild- eiji-aonuma-producteur-du-jeu-repond-a-nos-questions.htm

http://www.lemonde.fr/pixels/article/2017/01/21/jeux-video-legend-of-zelda-breath- of-the-wild-sera-un-moment-cle-dans-l-histoire-de-la-saga_5066750_4408996.html

http://fr.ign.com/the-legend-of-zelda-breath-of-the-wild-switch/22429/video/ interview-la-quete-du-progres-de-nintendo-pour-the-legend-of

https://www.gamekult.com/actualite/eiji-aonuma-un-zelda-ou-l-on-prend- plaisir-a-se-perdre-172637.html

http://www.ign.com/articles/2017/03/02/why-zelda-breath-of-the-wilds- touchscreen-features-were-cut

https://www.polygon.com/2017/3/10/14869766/zelda-breath-of-the-wild-link-hat

http://hitek.fr/actualite/breath-of-the-wild-details-bien-caches_12349

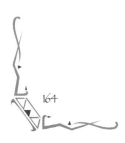

ARTICLES:

http://www.metacritic.com/game/switch/the-legend-of-zelda-breath-of-the-wild

http://www.metacritic.com/game/wii-u/the-legend-of-zelda-breath-of-the-wild

https://www.jvfrance.com/test-zelda-breath-of-the-wild-recap-notes-switch-wii-u-144415/

http://www.jeuxvideo.com/news/620274/20-20-a-zelda-la-note-decomplexee.htm

https://www.gamekult.com/emission/gamekult-l-emission-324-the-legend-of-zelda-breath-of-the-wild-3050793745.html

https://gamergen.com/tests/the-legend-of-zelda-breath-of-the-wild-nintendo-test-review-verdict-notes-280792-1

http://www.jeuxactu.com/test-zelda-breath-of-the-wild-sur-nintendo-switch-108281.htm

http://www.gameblog.fr/tests/2695-the-legend-of-zelda-breath-of-the-wild-switch

http://www.journaldugeek.com/tests/impressions-zelda-breath-of-the-wild-zelda-est-mort/

http://www.nintendoworldreport.com/news/44531/nintendo-sales-panic-march-2017-us-npd-group-results

https://venturebeat.com/2017/04/13/march-2017-npd-nintendo-sold-906000-switch-systems-last-month/

https://www.gamekult.com/actualite/le-million-pour-la-switch-au-japon-3050796669.html

https://www.gamekult.com/actualite/nous-on-peut-essayer-se-planter-corriger-et-recommencer-notre-interview-de-nintendo-3050796393.html

http://www.jeuxvideo.com/news/662288/nintendo-le-cours-en-bourse-bat-un-record-vieux-de-7-ans.htm *http://zelda.com/breath-of-the-wild/news/special-announcement-from-eiji-aonuma/*

http://www.ign.com/videos/2017/02/18/nintendo-voice-chat-ep-343-talking-1-2-switch-and-breath-of-the-wild-w-bill-trinen

http://www.siliconera.com/2017/02/20/nintendos-bill-trinen-explains-zelda-breath-wild-will-getting-dlc/

https://nintendowire.com/news/2017/02/20/nintendos-bill-trinen-talks-breath-wild-dlc/

http://www.extralife.fr/news-jv/14790/zelda-le-season-pass-mal.html

Speed runs and videos testing the game's limits:

http://www.zeldaspeedruns.com/leaderboards/botw/any
https://www.youtube.com/watch?v=S9MidlAD-k4
https://www.youtube.com/watch?v=X95IpnReaOQ
https://www.youtube.com/watch?v=0PrbroUjmDY
https://www.youtube.com/watch?v=tgddMie6EyA
https://www.youtube.com/watch?v=UGZElRJtyCo
https://www.youtube.com/watch?v=_gSb909-ovo
https://www.youtube.com/watch?v=EMdlqqL4pBk
https://www.youtube.com/watch?v=JJrynhrYZfw
https://www.youtube.com/watch?v=E2e_ajp_md8
https://www.youtube.com/watch?v=eEYqx39u3nI
https://www.youtube.com/watch?v=L_kglHaenv8

ZELDA

THE HISTORY OF A LEGENDARY SAGA
VOLUME 2: BREATH OF THE WILD

TABLE OF CONTENTS

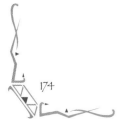